KT-412-182

AMERICA IN WORLD AFFAIRS

By

ALLAN NEVINS

*Harmsworth Professor of American History
in the University of Oxford, 1940–41*

WORKING MEN'S COLLEGE LIBRARY

OXFORD UNIVERSITY PRESS
LONDON · NEW YORK · TORONTO
1941

OXFORD   UNIVERSITY   PRESS

AMEN HOUSE, E.C.4

London Edinburgh Glasgow New York
Toronto Melbourne Capetown Bombay
Calcutta Madras

HUMPHREY   MILFORD

PUBLISHER TO THE UNIVERSITY

PRINTED IN GREAT BRITAIN

CONTENTS

ILLUSTRATIONS

MAPS

AMERICA BETWEEN THE OCEANS

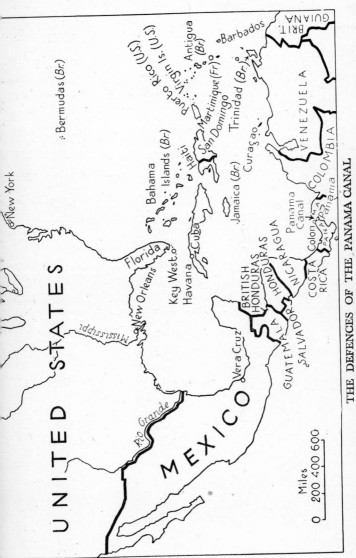

THE DEFENCES OF THE PANAMA CANAL

FOR SUPPLEMENTARY READING

James Truslow Adams: *An American Looks at the British Empire.*[1]
William Agar: *Food or Freedom: The Vital Blockade.*[1]
Frederick B. Artz: *1917 and 1941.*[1]
Charles A. Beard: *The Devil Theory of War.*
Samuel Flagg Bemis: *A Diplomatic History of the United States.*
Stephen Vincent Benét: *A Summons to the Free.*[1]
Edwin Borchard and William Potter Lage: *Neutrality for the United States.*
Phillips Bradley: *Can We Stay Out of War?*
D. W. Brogan: *American Foreign Policy.*[2]
Allen W. Dulles and Hamilton Fish Armstrong: *Can We Be Neutral?*
Denna Frank Fleming: *The United States and the League of Nations, 1918–1920.*
—— *The United States and World Organization, 1920–1933.*
Grayson Kirk: *The Monroe Doctrine Today.*[1]
Walter Millis: *The Road to War: America, 1914–1917.*
—— *The Faith of An American.*[1]
Samuel Eliot Morison and Henry Steele Commager: *The Growth of the American Republic.*
Franklin D. Roosevelt: *Mr. Roosevelt Speaks.*[1]
Charles Seymour: *American Neutrality, 1914–1917.*
Benjamin H. Williams: *American Diplomacy, Policies and Practice.*

[1] Pamphlets—*America Faces the War* series (Oxford University Press).
[2] *Oxford Pamphlets on World Affairs* (O.U.P.).

CHAPTER I

TRADITIONS AND PRINCIPLES

AMBASSADOR GEORGE HARVEY is alleged once to have made the absurd remark that "the traditional American foreign policy is to have no foreign policy". The fact is that the United States has always had a foreign policy —though not always a good one. Like other nations, it has acted in the main upon motives of self-interest. Its course in foreign affairs has sometimes conduced to the peace, prosperity, and well-being of the world as a whole, and has repeatedly been generous and disinterested. It has sometimes been timid, evasive, and destructively selfish. The key to its policy is always to be found partly in considerations of immediate expediency, and partly in American tradition.

For several reasons, tradition counts for a great deal. The United States is now more than 160 years old, it has had a far longer continuous life under the present form of government than any important nation of continental Europe, and it has had time to develop a distinct national personality. Its people have always been highly conscious of its history and of what they believe its historic mission to be. Then, too, the nation has been protected from forces which would bring about rapid deviations and fluctuations in its foreign policy. Because of its size, power, and relatively safe position, it has not had to take account of minor changes in foreign capitals, and has seen little reason to fear sudden crises. It has therefore normally been easier to predict what course America would take in given circumstances than what the French, Germans, Russians, or Japanese would do. Finally, the general stability and conservatism of the American Government have made for a distinct stability and conservatism in foreign relations.

The American people like to believe that in ordinary times they take slight interest in external affairs; that, standing apart from the quarrelsome family of Old World nations, they care little about what occurs beyond their borders. Many of them have been complacent and even boastful about this attitude. Beyond question, indifference to the rest of the world used to be widespread. It was not creditable to the citizens of the wealthy, powerful, and supposedly alert republic. One of its roots lay in sheer ignorance of other peoples, an ignorance especially noticeable in frontier communities. Another root was embedded in a certain pharisaical Fourth-of-July sense of superiority over breeds of men who had not been wise enough to adopt republican institutions and democratic modes of life, and who seemed inferior to Americans in business hustle. Still another source was to be found in a feeling of apprehension with regard to European leaders and diplomats; they were thought to be too sophisticated, astute, and unscrupulous to be trusted by Americans, and the wisest course was to ignore them.

Yet this indifference can easily be over-stated. In every generation many Americans have felt a passionate interest in international politics. This was natural in a nation of newspaper readers, generally literate if not highly educated; a nation drawn from diverse sources, and maintaining numerous contacts with the lands of their various origins, a nation placed midway between Europe and the Orient, looking both east and west. In Washington's day the masses were intensely aroused by the conflict between Britain and France. In Madison's time the American people were sucked into the final convulsion of the Napoleonic Wars. In Monroe's time they were powerfully stirred by the Latin-American and Greek struggles for independence. So the story might be pursued down to the present day. The second officer of government, so far as practical power and prestige go, has nearly always been the Secretary of State—*i.e.*, the officer in charge of foreign affairs.

Moreover, a great change took place in 1914. Before that year Americans were able to forget foreign affairs for considerable intervals. Wilson's first inaugural speech in 1913 contained not a line on the subject, and his message to Congress the following December referred only briefly to Bryan's "cooling-off"[1] treaties and Huerta's usurpations in Mexico. But since 1914 Americans have been far more

---

[1] These were treaties binding the contracting parties not to go to war for the year during which the dispute was being investigated by a committee set up by the treaties. In this year of grace it was hoped that passions would cool off.

conscious of the outside world. They have set up important agencies for their systematic study. Notable among these are the Council on Foreign Relations, a select body which maintains an admirable library in New York, holds meetings like those of Chatham House in London, sponsors valuable books, and issues the quarterly *Foreign Affairs*; and the Foreign Policy Association, which, with headquarters in New York and branches elsewhere, operates on a broader level of public education. A survey about 1930 of organizations for the study of international relations showed that more than 1200 then claimed a considerable membership. In addition, such agencies as the Federation of Women's Clubs, League of Women Voters, Rotary, Kiwanis, and various church bodies, have given an increasing place in their activities to the study of foreign affairs, while universities and colleges have offered more and more courses. Important new libraries like the Hoover Library at Stanford (devoted primarily to the first World War) have been established, while existing libraries have been enriched with new resources.

All this, with the increased space given in American newspapers to such able foreign correspondents as Edgar Mowrer, John Whitaker, and William Chamberlain, and with the growing attention of radio commentators to foreign news, has had a salutary effect. It has tended to break down a parochialism that was unworthy and crippling. Woodrow Wilson asserted in 1916 that "America, which ought to have had the broadest vision of any nation, has raised up an extraordinary number of provincial thinkers . . . men who thought that the United States was not ready to take her competitive part in the struggle for peaceful conquest of the world". He had reason later to know that he had spoken truly. The provincialism still exists. As it diminishes, American foreign policy can be altered for the better.

Particularly can it be improved in details; it can be made more positive and constructive, and, where the world-situation permits, less timid and more boldly altruistic. The broad principles of American policy are not going to be easy to change. Powerful groups will oppose any change at all, and alterations will have to come slowly if at all. These principles fit the American character, and on the whole have served the nation well. Like all basic principles of national conduct, they have their merits and their faults and their value depends largely on how they are applied.

The cardinal tradition or principle of the United States in ordering its foreign relations has been its predilection for the promotion of democracy throughout the world. The republic was born with the sense of a national mission. That mission was to assist in the diffusion of popular government. Imbued with this feeling, America has always been ready to denounce despotisms, dictatorships, and all forms of repression. The same sentiment that nerved the patriots of 1776 to resist George III inspired Daniel Webster to defy the despotism of Austria, Wilson to draw the sword against the autocracy of the German Empire, and Franklin D. Roosevelt to assail the tyranny of the totalitarian states. The Government was nearly always quick to recognize republics set up by popular revolt, as in South America, nearly always glad to welcome rebels like Kossuth, and nearly always ready to send a word of cheer to oppressed peoples.

Historically, the attitude behind this tradition has undergone certain changes. During the first generation of the republic American leaders were somewhat defiantly conscious that it was an experiment. As the experiment succeeded, they came to regard the nation as a great beacon light, a shining exemplar of democratic institutions in a generally benighted world. Lincoln expressed this sentiment at Gettysburg, when he said that government of the people, by the people, for the people was undergoing the supreme trial which would prove its undying worth. Later on, and especially when Wilson assumed national leadership, a host of Americans took a more crusading attitude; not merely by their example, but by their armed might, they would see the world made safe for democracy. It can be predicted that the United States will always show a strong hostility to autocratic movements, and an impassioned sympathy with democratic tendencies; and that when necessity arises it will become, as in 1914–18 and 1939–41, an arsenal for the protection of democracy overseas.

One facet of this predilection for democracy is a somewhat naïve belief in the democratic management of international relations. Americans have repeatedly expressed the faith

I. ROYAL VISIT TO THE U.S.A.

1. AT THE PRESIDENT'S HOME
   (*Wide World Photos.*)

2. DRIVING WITH THE PRESIDENT
   (*Wide World Photos.*)

3. AT WASHINGTON'S TOMB
   (*Wide World Photos.*)

that peoples dislike war, and that only unrepresentative leaders carry nations into conflict. This idea shows a defective knowledge both of history and of the nature of government. Nevertheless, it is widely held. Associated with it is a dislike of secret diplomacy as connected with aristocratic and irresponsible governments. The first of Wilson's Fourteen Points in 1918 called for the abolition of secret diplomacy. Though some basis for this attitude obviously exists, Wilson soon found that if he pushed his demand for open covenants openly arrived at too far, he made the practical work of international negotiation quite impossible.

Another fixed principle of American policy is the avoidance of needless entanglements with foreign nations. It is incorrect to say that the United States has generally pursued an isolationist policy. It has frequently done the precise opposite. But the nation *has* followed the general lines of Washington's oft-misquoted advice in his Farewell Address. He wrote: "The great rule of conduct for us in regard to foreign nations is, in extending our commercial relations, to have as little political connection as possible." He pointed out that Europe had a set of primary interests alien to those of America and fell into frequent controversies the causes of which did not concern the United States. "Hence, therefore, it must be unwise in us to implicate ourselves by artificial ties in the ordinary vicissitudes of her politics." But he said nothing about entangling alliances, a phrase coined later by Jefferson. Indeed, although he warned his countrymen against permanent alliances, Washington specifically declared that they might "safely trust to temporary alliances for extraordinary purposes". He also made it clear that his predominant motive in counselling a cautious policy was "to gain time to our country to settle and mature its yet recent institutions". In short, he was for a reasonable avoidance of political connections with other lands, especially during the infancy of the republic, but he was not a dogmatic isolationist.

And, with some aberrations, America has followed the prudent policy defined by Washington. In its earliest years the nation made an alliance with France. It has recently made a practical defensive alliance with Canada. It has participated in three world-wide wars, those of 1812, 1917, and 1940. It annexed the Philippine archipelago far across the Pacific, and took a historic stand as defender of the Open Door in China. Its sailors under Preble and Decatur fought to suppress the Barbary pirates; its soldiers and marines a century later took part in suppressing the Boxer rebellion in China. It sent a squadron to Japan which by treaty opened that country to Western civilization. Its representatives played a leading rôle in the First Hague Conference in 1899, and again in the Second Hague Conference in 1907. It has never been an isolated nation. But its people have always tried to avoid alliances, entanglements, and conflicts in the Old World, and have sharply limited their commitments there.

Unfortunately, many Americans have made a fetish of the idea of isolationism. Instead of applying the rule of common sense and recognizing their modern position in an interdependent world, they have erected John Adams's and Jefferson's warnings against foreign embroilments into a towering barrier. Active participation in the affairs of mankind for the common good need not be an entanglement. Instead of leading to peril, expense, and war, it may avert them. Men can travel more rapidly between New York and London today than between New York and Philadelphia under Washington; America and Brazil have more mutual dependence on each other now than Massachusetts and Connecticut had then. Americans are slow to realize this, just as they are slow to comprehend that the United States is no longer a weak nation, but the world's greatest Power. They will not admit that it should play a world rôle proportionate to its wealth and might.

A third guiding principle of American foreign policy is the Monroe Doctrine, with which we may couple the idea of Pan-Americanism. The Doctrine, promulgated when in 1823 Latin America seemed in danger of attack from a reactionary European combination, laid down two firm rules. These were, first, that the two American continents were no longer to be considered subject to colonization by any European nation; and second, that any interference with the new Latin-American republics for the purpose of controlling or oppressing them would be regarded as an unfriendly act towards the United States. It is clear that the

Doctrine possesses great latitude. It could be used to stop a wide variety of undertakings by European Powers.

For example, any attempt by Italy, Japan, or Germany to establish a political connection with the host of Italians, Japanese, and Germans who have migrated to South America—to treat them as colonists—would meet determined resistance from the United States. Similarly, any attempt by an Axis Power to use economic pressure, political propaganda, or fifth-column activities to "control" or "oppress" a Latin-American country would violate the Doctrine as clearly as the landing of an army. The ordinary American thinks of the Doctrine in vague terms. He has probably never read its text, and looks upon it simply as a general "Hands off!" warning. But he is convinced that it is one of the bulwarks of American safety, and will tolerate no meddling with it. A familiar story tells of the citizen who remarked: "I don't know precisely what the Doctrine is, but I would gladly die in its defence!"

In its original form, and during the period when the Latin-American republics were growing to vigour, the Monroe Doctrine was necessary and wise. It benefited these republics by keeping them free from the intrigues and forays of rival European Powers. It benefited the United States by protecting its southern flank. But the Doctrine was unfortunately given much too wide an interpretation by some Presidents, and stretched at times to cover improper objects. Moreover, as Argentina, Brazil, and Chile reached mature strength, they resented the protectorate which the Doctrine offered. The defence of the hemisphere, they maintained, should be the business not of Uncle Sam, but of all the republics acting jointly.

One of various unhappy extensions of the Monroe Doctrine was furnished by the generally liberal-minded President Cleveland. He laid down the rule that if a European Power holding New World territory had a boundary dispute with a Latin-American republic which it would not or could not settle by friendly means, then the United States had a right to step in and adjust the boundary. Another extension or "corollary" was invented by Theodore Roosevelt. He declared that whenever the Government of a Latin-American nation became so disorderly, dishonest, or oppressive that European Powers might be provoked to interfere on behalf of their nationals, then the United States (since it forbade any European interference) ought itself to exercise an international police power. This Roosevelt Corollary provided a cloak for very dubious interventions. Another extension came from the Senate in 1912. It passed a resolution asserting that no non-American "corporation or association" could be permitted to acquire an American harbour if it were so situated that naval or military forces there might threaten the United States. This was aimed at Japanese interests supposedly eyeing Magdalena Bay in Mexico.

All these and other extensions have proved but temporary. The Monroe Doctrine has now for years been restricted to something like its original limits. Under Franklin D. Roosevelt steps have been taken to make it multinational. But it still contains very sharp teeth, as any European adventurers would quickly find.

The central object of Pan-Americanism has no necessary connection with the Monroe Doctrine. It is a movement intended to bring the American republics into closer association for the promotion of trade, cultural interests, peace, and security. Of recent years leaders of the United States have favoured the inclusion of Canada in the Pan-American system. But although the ideal of Pan-Americanism dates back to the time of Henry Clay, it has made slow and discouraging progress.

One obstacle lies in the fact that Latin America has always possessed much stronger ties, cultural, moral, and economic, with Continental Europe than with the United States. Another difficulty long lay in the deep suspicion with which the United States was regarded by her southern neighbours. The Mexican War and the filibustering expeditions in the fifties seemed proof of a predatory habit. After Theodore Roosevelt "took" Panama, Yankee imperialism was widely feared. Even today, despite the reassuring policy of Herbert Hoover and Franklin D. Roosevelt, some latent distrust exists. A third obstacle is the pronounced difference in governmental ideals. While the people of the United States detest dictatorships, many South American countries have found them best adapted to their particular stage of political progress. The consequence is that in various Pan-American Conferences it has

B (N.)

been difficult to find a common ground in discussing political aims. Finally, and fundamentally, the mind and temperament of the Latin-American differ radically from those of English-speaking Americans. Yankees tend to regard their southern neighbours with amused contempt as indolent, unstable, and unprogressive; Chileans and Argentines tend to look on North Americans as materialistic, irreligious, and unscrupulously aggressive.

The early Pan-American Conference accomplished little. The first was opened in Washington (1889) by Secretary Blaine, who hoped for an American *zollverein*, a customs union which would increase hemispheric trade and curtail that with Europe. He also advocated the drafting of a plan for arbitrating all disputes. Both proposals were voted down, for mutual jealousies and distrust of the United States made them impracticable. The second and third conferences failed to advance the arbitration proposals; for while Argentina led a group which believed in compulsory arbitration, the United States, Mexico, and Brazil would accept only voluntary arbitration. The fourth conference in 1910 dealt only with secondary questions. When the fifth conference met in Santiago in 1923, most Latin-American nations belonged to the League, while the United States did not; strong feeling had been kindled in South America by the intervention of Washington in several Caribbean republics; and Mexico and the United States were at loggerheads on important issues. As a result, the meeting proved abortive. When Dr. Brum of Uruguay proposed a continentalization of the Monroe Doctrine, the American delegates flatly rejected the idea. No agreement was reached as to arbitration. In all, the conference contrasted very unfavourably with what Europe was then accomplishing at Locarno and Geneva.

Nevertheless, the Pan-American idea did possess genuine vitality, and of late it has proved more fruitful. The sixth conference was opened at Havana in 1928 by President Coolidge in person, and produced good feeling if little else. Five years later the seventh conference, held at Montevideo, gave the Roosevelt Administration its first opportunity to expound the Good Neighbour policy. A declaration that "No state has the right to intervene in the internal or external affairs of another" was cordially supported by Secretary Hull, and unanimously adopted. The eighth conference, held in Lima in 1938, was overshadowed by the threat of a new World War. Secretary Hull, fearing that the Axis Powers would effect a dangerous penetration of South America, was anxious to build up a united front against international aggressors. Argentina placed herself in opposition to any drastic action. But the Declaration of Lima, adopted unanimously, did affirm the twenty-one nations' faith in democracy, and did pledge them to consultation and at least a measure of common action if any was menaced by external threat.

Pan-Americanism has thus, after many disappointments, accomplished something for concord and security in the Western hemisphere, and fostered closer commercial and cultural relations. It proved ineffective as long as the Latin American States could reasonably fear armed intervention or economic aggression by the United States. When Washington became able to promise a liberal attitude, it proved effective. It has laid foundations on which an imposing structure may yet be built.

A fourth basic principle of American foreign policy has been freedom to navigate the seas in peace or war. It was made the second of Wilson's Fourteen Points; it has been resolutely upheld at all times except in two great crises—when Jefferson persuaded Congress in 1807 to pass the Embargo, and when Congress in 1935-37 passed laws giving up certain maritime rights. Both steps were taken in a desperate effort to keep the United States out of a worldwide conflict. Both failed. Secretary of War Henry L. Stimson in May, 1941, described the neutrality legislation of 1935-37 as "a violation of our most sacred and important tradition in foreign policy, the freedom of the seas"; Secretary of the Navy Frank Knox called it a "terrible blunder". But apart from these two interludes, America has vigorously maintained the principle.

The reason is simple. The United States has always been a strong mercantile nation, possessing an immense merchant fleet down to the Civil War, and one of considerable strength after the World War. Foreign trade has been important to its economy. It has repeatedly been the principal neutral in a war-torn world. It has naturally stood for the right to send its goods and ships to every part of the globe without intolerable restrictions and seizures by belligerent Powers. The Declaration of Paris in 1856 embodied a set of peculiarly American principles, for which the United States had contended ever since 1776. Only disagreement on one point, the abolition of privateering, prevented Washington from accepting the Declaration. The historic American doctrines were that the neutral flag covers all goods except contraband of war; that neutral goods, when not contraband, are not subject to seizure even though carried by an enemy ship; and that a blockade must be effective in order to be binding, and must be maintained with due respect to the lives of neutrals. The Declaration of London of 1909 similarly embodied rules and definitions which corresponded with American views.

It was largely in vindication of the freedom of the seas that the United States fought the War of 1812. It was largely for the same reason that it entered the World War in 1917. The country should have clung more rigidly to the principle. Stimson in 1941 said that he regarded its abandonment by the neutrality legislation of 1935–37 as a tragic mistake; and events had proved him right. But while Congress may impose voluntary limitations upon American maritime rights, it will not accept limitations dictated by others. On this point the American position was forcibly stated by Wilson in 1917: "Once accept a single abatement of right, and many other humiliations would certainly follow, and the whole fine fabric of international law might crumble under our hands piece by piece."

Another facet of the same tradition is America's insistence upon the Open Door, and upon the abolition of discriminations in maritime facilities. The Open Door in China was first proposed by the British Government. But Secretary John Hay took up the idea, pressed it upon other Powers, and made it a temporary success. In general terms, Americans mean by the Open Door the right to sell goods, maintain industries, and make investments in any land on an equal footing with other foreigners. The principle applies to every nation, not merely China. Any discrimination by Argentina or Switzerland in favour of Germans or Britons over Americans would arouse American indignation. In China, custodianship of the Open Door was handed over to a whole group of nations by the Nine-Power Treaty of 1922. They have failed to keep it open, but most Americans regard the defeat of this policy as merely temporary.

When the United States became independent, it found its trade hampered by the mercantilist restrictions of many nations, and set itself to clear away as much of this jungle growth as possible. The Netherlands, for example, until 1852 refused to admit American vessels into the Dutch colonies in the New World. Various nations imposed lower tonnage dues on home ships than foreign ships, placed lower tariffs upon goods carried in national ships, and set up discriminations of other types. Ever since 1783 the United States has combated the international practice of such discriminations. By reciprocal legislation or formal treaty, by 1860 it had brought about the cessation of nearly all in direct trade, and a great part of them in indirect trade. America had thus made a signal contribution to the death of mercantilism and to freedom of world intercourse.

In dealing with tariffs, the United States has also consistently opposed discriminations. The ordinary provision of commercial treaties has been, in substance, that "the two parties shall enjoy in the ports of each other, in regard to commerce and navigation, the privileges of the most-favoured nation". Many treaties of the nineteenth century were upon a conditional most-favoured-nation basis. That is, they provided on both sides for certain special rates which, being based on special bargains, did not automatically extend to other nations. But if these other nations made similar concessions, they could obtain the special rates; so that the treaties were not really discriminatory. The principal recent definition of American policy is offered by the Reciprocal Tariff Act of 1934. This permitted the President for three years (a term twice renewed) to negotiate trade agreements with other nations, reducing existing duties up to 50 per cent.; and it extended gratuitously to all nations (unless they discriminated against the United States) every advantage offered by any reciprocal trade bargain. Discrimination was thus completely ruled out.

All in all, the United States has stood for unfettered freedom of commercial intercourse throughout the world. Since the Civil War it has set up high tariffs—often egregiously high. It has never denied the right of other nations to establish such tariffs. But it has insisted that they should apply to all alike except as modified by reciprocal bargains; it has opposed discriminatory port and navigation laws. Needless to say, it has been sternly hostile to barter arrangements of the type set up by the totalitarian Powers, the essence of which is discrimination and privilege. The third of Wilson's Fourteen Points called for the removal of economic barriers between nations, and he was simply enunciating an old American doctrine.

So far as it has been guided by these basic principles—predilection for democracy, avoidance of needless entanglements, the Monroe Doctrine, the removal of commercial barriers—the foreign policy of the United States has been a mixture of caution and old-fashioned liberalism. The desire to support democracy, shown so vigorously in Clay's recognition of the new South American republics, in Webster's letter to Baron Hulsemann denouncing Austrian tyranny, and in a thousand other occurrences down to Roosevelt's attempts to check Hitler and Mussolini, is a liberal desire. The spirit of Pan-Americanism is a liberal spirit. America's belief in the Open Door and in freedom of the seas is a liberal belief. The spirit of Washington's warning about avoiding "artificial ties" and the "ordinary vicissitudes" of the Old World was a cautious spirit. The primary motive for the Monroe Doctrine was a defensive or cautious motive.

But there have been darker phases in American policy, and it would falsify the picture not to indicate them. The United States has often played a creditable and even gallant rôle in world affairs; but it has sometimes played an exceedingly selfish and even predatory part. Its caution has occasionally degenerated into outright timidity.

The policy of territorial expansion which was aggressively followed until 1853 involved some unhappy episodes. On the whole, expansion to the Pacific was so inevitable and healthful that the term "manifest destiny" could well be applied to it. No objection could be entered to the Louisiana purchase, or to the peaceful settlement of the Oregon boundary which gave the United States the North-west up to the 49th parallel. The annexation of Texas, at least as far as the Nueces, was also a defensible act. But the Mexican War proved to be a predatory war; and the annexation of the whole northern third of what had been Mexico could be justified only on the Carlylean principle that might and right are interchangeable terms. One motive behind the War of 1812 was the desire to seize Canadian soil, and American armies invaded Canada with intentions that were distinctly acquisitive.

Fortunately, after the Civil War the expansionist spirit fell into decay. An effort by President Grant to bring about the annexation of Santo Domingo was condemned by public opinion and effectively resisted by the Senate. To be sure, the United States in 1867 did purchase Alaska from Russia. But it was part of the North American continent, was virtually unpopulated, and was a natural appendage of the United States. An effort by Republican leaders to extend a protectorate over Nicaragua in 1884–85 was sharply halted when Cleveland became President in the latter year. A similar effort in 1892–93 to annex Hawaii was again halted by Cleveland's return to office. During the entire period from the Civil War to the Spanish War the American people seemed convinced that they should annex no territory outside the continent, no territory occupied by people of alien blood, language, and traditions, and no territory that had to be taken by force. Most Americans thought the national domain complete.

But expansionist tendencies revived at the close of the century. The partitioning of Africa by the European Powers had aroused in many Americans a desire for empire. Captain A. T. Mahan, "the naval philosopher of the new imperialism", preached not only the importance of sea-power, but the duty of carrying civilization overseas. "Comparative religion teaches that creeds which reject missionary enterprise are foredoomed to decay", he wrote. "May it not be so with nations? . . . How much poorer would the world have been, had England heeded the cautious hesitancy that now bids us reject every advance beyond our shores." These sentiments fell pleasingly upon the ears of rising politicians like Theodore Roosevelt and Henry Cabot Lodge. The growth of a sensational Press, with William Randolph Hearst as its worst and Joseph Pulitzer as its best exemplar, strengthened the appetite for an exciting foreign policy. Many Protestants liked the idea of carrying religious light to heathen (or Catholic) areas. A feeling grew up among manufacturers and exporters that trade would follow the flag into new areas.

Under the spell of Mahan and his own belief in a virile national policy, Roosevelt as Assistant-Secretary of the Navy in 1898 seized a day when the Secretary was absent, and ordered the Far-Eastern squadron which Dewey commanded at Hong-Kong to be ready to descend upon Manila if war with Spain began. "The very devil seemed to possess him", John D. Long, Secretary of the Navy, wrote of Roosevelt. The battle of Manila Bay was the sequel of that order. The annexation of the Philippines was the sequel of the battle. McKinley hesitated whether to take nothing, to take Luzon alone, or to take the whole archipelago. But reflection, prayer, and a western tour to sound out public sentiment impelled him to a clean sweep. As E. L. Godkin put it: "God told Duty to tell Destiny to tell McKinley" to take all the islands.

At the same time Puerto Rico was annexed, while Cuba was placed under a virtual protectorate. Hawaii had already been taken over. The election of 1900, fought out upon imperialism as the "paramount" issue, seemed to give the new policy an emphatic endorsement. Before Theodore Roosevelt had been long in office, Panama was also an American protectorate, and ready for the building of the isthmian canal.

The motives of the American people in this sudden expansion overseas were mixed. In so far as the United States was actuated by a desire to help take up the white man's burden in backward areas and to teach Christianity to pagan peoples, the impulse was good. In so far as the nation was actuated by jingoism, a feeling that it ought to boss some subject peoples, and a wish to swagger before other world Powers, its course was bad. But the experiment was to be judged by results; and the nation soon decided that imperialism had been a mistake. Assurances of eventual independence were given the Filipinos by Democrats and Republicans alike, notably in the Jones Act of 1916. They had a solid basis in American feeling that the Filipinos would be troublesome wards, and in a realization that, as Theodore Roosevelt soon admitted, the islands were strategically an Achilles heel. Finally, the hostility of American farmers to Philippine agricultural exports led to decisive action. In

1934 Congress provided for independence after a ten-year probationary period.

Under Franklin D. Roosevelt also the virtual protectorate over Cuba embodied in the Platt Amendment was abrogated. Most Americans would have been glad to find an honourable way to terminate their responsibility for overcrowded, poverty-stricken Puerto Rico. The imperialist adventure had unquestionably resulted in a genuine contribution by the United States to world order and civilization. The conquest of yellow fever in Cuba was but one of many striking achievements. Filipinos, Cubans, and Puerto Ricans were far better off for the tutelage they had received. But by 1940 most Americans wanted no more such adventures.

Another highly unfortunate policy which the United States pursued intermittently from 1900 down to 1929 was military or naval intervention to maintain order in the Caribbean republics. It can be said that some intervention was an absolute necessity. The United States quite properly felt anxious to protect its isthmian lifeline. The safety of the Panama Canal is absolutely vital to a nation which faces strong potential foes in both Atlantic and Pacific without a two-ocean navy. Philander C. Knox pointed out in a speech while Secretary of State that the canal had made "the safety, the peace, and the prosperity of Central America and the zone of the Caribbean of paramount interest", essential to the American Government; and that it was precisely in this belt that "the malady of revolutions and financial collapse" was most dangerous. It was probably necessary at times that the United States should police the little island republics of Haiti and Santo Domingo, and one or more of the Central American States. But under Taft, Wilson, and Harding the interference was carried much too far.

The results were summed up by one caustic American historian in 1927: "In about thirty years, we have created two new republics—Cuba and Panama; converted both of them and three other Latin-American countries—the Dominican Republic, Nicaragua, and Haiti—into virtual protectorates; intervened by force at least thirty times in the internal affairs of nine supposedly sovereign and independent nations; made the period of intervention last anywhere from a few days to a dozen years; enlarged our investments from a paltry two or three hundred millions of dollars to the tidy sum of upwards of three billions; and installed in four states our own collector of customs to insure payment." He might have added that the interventions had deeply alarmed all Latin America. For South American opinion rapidly came to the view that unilateral intervention for economic reasons was unjustifiable; that only collective intervention for humanitarian reasons could be approved.

It was the intervention in Nicaragua, Haiti, and Santo Domingo which most disturbed liberal elements in the United States and outside. For years Nicaragua suffered under a contumacious dictator named Zelaya. His general attitude towards foreigners was summed up in an alleged boast: "I ridicule the United States, laugh at Germany, spit on England." Not without reason, when a revolt against him broke out in 1909 Washington lent moral and physical support to the revolutionists. They set up a new Government. The United States then reorganized the Nicaraguan finances, placed an American agent in charge of the collection of customs, and asked the Government to refund a British debt by borrowing money from American bankers. When Nicaragua showed reluctance, a warship was sent to the coast—and ratification of the loan soon followed. But political disturbances continued. The United States intervened in 1912 to end them, and kept a force of marines continuously at the Nicaraguan capital until 1925. Already Theodore Roosevelt had placed a Receiver-General of Customs in Santo Domingo.

When Woodrow Wilson became President in 1913 he made a series of statements condemning intervention, especially in behalf of any "special group of interests". Yet in the end he ordered more armed interferences than any other President. In Mexico, he refused to recognize the bloodstained Huerta as President, and under provocation captured Vera Cruz. With the help of Argentina, Brazil, and Chile, who offered their service as mediators, he then forced Huerta out of power and recognized Carranza as his successor. Wilson also sent armed forces into Haiti in 1915. Once more he could plead a very considerable justification in events; for a long series of disturbances had culminated in a bloody massacre of political prisoners by the President, who was thereupon lynched by a frenzied mob. Washington

ared that some European nation might exploit the dis-
rder, and American bayonets soon gleamed in the capital.
Iaiti was forced to accept a Constitution which made her a
irtual protectorate. In 1920 Franklin D. Roosevelt, then
assistant-Secretary of the Navy, made his famous boast:
You know I have had something to do with running a
ouple of little republics. The facts are that I wrote Haiti's
Constitution myself, and if I do say it, I think it's a pretty
ood Constitution."

Yet Wilson made his dislike for the principle of interven-
ion clear even while using the method. Public sentiment
nmistakably grew more unfavourable to it. As isolationist
eeling rose after the World War, Americans showed them-
elves opposed to sending their sons to help fight guerrilla
vars in little tropical republics. "Imperialism" had be-
ome unpopular. President Coolidge took the marines out
f Nicaragua in 1925. Then the next year, as disorders
roke out again, he sent them back. He soon had some
,000 troops in the little republic. A storm of criticism burst
bout his head. "Oh Monroe Doctrine!" cried a Demo-
ratic Congressman, "how many crimes have been com-
aitted in thy name!" Coolidge had to explain that "We
re not making war on Nicaragua any more than a police-
nan on the street is making war on passers-by". Stimson,
oing to the scene of trouble, succeeded in working out a
eaceful solution. And when Hoover came in, he made the
bandonment of interventionism a cardinal policy. Armed
orces in all the little republics were reduced, and control
vas turned over to the local governments as rapidly as was
easible.

On the whole, it is not unfair to say that intervention in
he Caribbean was only a temporary policy, produced by
he excessive disorderliness of half a dozen republics in the
ears 1900–1930, and by the somewhat exaggerated fear of
Americans that their vital Panama route might somehow be
ndangered. The intervention policy will not revive unless
he disorderliness and the fear revive together. And even if
hat happens, future interventions are likely to be on the
ollective basis favoured by Latin America.

It need not be said that both American expansion and
American intervention had prominent economic aspects.
ndeed, all American foreign policy has had its economic

background and implications. The promotion of a nation
commerce and protection of its investments, within th
limits of equity, are among the primary reasons why foreig
offices, consulates, and embassies exist. That the Unite
States has gone beyond equitable bounds more frequentl
than other great nations no one believes. It was in the da
of "dollar diplomacy" that it pushed economic considera
tions to their fullest extent; and these days were fortunatel
short.

The term "dollar diplomacy" is specially associated wit
the Taft Administration, 1908–13. By it is meant a systema
tic effort by the State Department to help American capit
to flow into areas which it would not otherwise enter. It wa
in the Far East that Taft and Knox pursued "dollar d
plomacy" most actively. Their major motive was purel
materialistic—to foster trade and to encourage safe capit
investment. But they had also a commendable minor objec
the strengthening of China's political integrity. This wa
particularly prominent in the mind of Willard Straight, wh
as consul-general at Mukden under Theodore Roosevel
became alarmed by Japanese penetration, and decided tha
if the United States put more money into the Far East
would be in a better position to maintain the Open Doo
The State Department tried to push American bankin
interests into important railway enterprises in the Orien
but it accomplished little except to irritate Japan.

"Dollar diplomacy" was also conspicuously applied t
Central America. There again the economic motive wa
perhaps paramount. But a political object, the safeguardin
of the isthmian route, was also prominent. Economic back
wardness, the depressions which gave birth to revolutio
and financial instability all invited European interferenc
If American bankers, traders, fruit-companies, and railroa
builders made Central America prosperous and financiall
stable, they had done something not only for their ow
pocket-books, but also for the security of the canal; so Kno
argued. Indeed, he said they had done something fo
"suffering humanity". But the policy actually led to de
mands, backed by a threat of force, for selfish privilege
American opinion was always chilly towards it. The treatie
which Knox negotiated with Nicaragua and Honduras fo
refunding their debts under the guidance of America

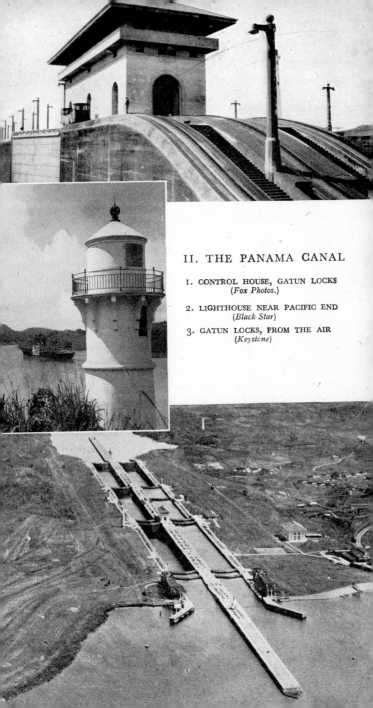

II. THE PANAMA CANAL

1. CONTROL HOUSE, GATUN LOCKS
   (*Fox Photos.*)

2. LIGHTHOUSE NEAR PACIFIC END
   (*Black Star*)

3. GATUN LOCKS, FROM THE AIR
   (*Keystone*)

bankers were defeated by the Senate. When Woodrow Wilson came to power in 1913, he explicitly repudiated "dollar diplomacy". It was not wholly dead, and Wilson himself did something to keep it alive both in Nicaragua and China, working hand in hand with the bankers. But it has remained under general condemnation, and since the World War is but a memory.

All in all, "dollar diplomacy" in flagrant form endured for less than a decade. The real charge to be brought against American foreign policy on economic grounds is that it has not seldom been confused and blundering.

It was folly for the United States after the World War, for example, to demand payment of the heavy war debts while raising a steep tariff wall. The Government had lent the Allies in 1917–18 a total of $7,077,114,000 in cash, and after the Armistice a total of $3,273,364,000 in cash and supplies. The debtor nations correctly asserted that they could not pay in gold, because Europe did not possess enough of the metal, and because they needed gold to support their own currencies. They wished to pay through goods and services. But first by the Fordney–McCumber Act, and in 1930 by the outrageous Smoot–Hawley Act, the United States built insuperable commercial barriers. A diplomat entering New York harbour was asked what he thought of the towering skyscrapers. "They make me think of your tariff," he replied. These tariffs provoked a series of retaliatory measures, including the Ottawa Agreements, and contributed heavily to the economic anarchy of the next decade. But they also conflicted sharply with the debt policy and the agricultural policy of the nation.

Under Harding, an indefensibly hard bargain was driven with the principal debtor, Great Britain. The loans made had aggregated $4,277,000,000. It was agreed that payment should be spread over sixty-two years, with interest at the high average rate of 3·3 per cent. Coolidge set his face sternly against any cancellation of principal. "They hired the money, didn't they?" he demanded. Though the French were given a far better interest rate, 1·6 per cent., and the Italians the low rate of 0·4 per cent., the principal in all instances was left untouched. For some years European nations found the problem of making debt payments over the tariff difficult, but were assisted by the large loans which

Americans sent to Germany, and which then went in part to the Allied nations as reparations. Finally, when the great depression began to stifle the world, debt-payment across the Smoot-Hawley wall became absolutely impossible.

The short-sighted economic nationalism of the American tariff also gravely injured the farming interest. It reduced the European market for agricultural commodities while it raised the price of many manufactured products which the farmer had to buy. Rural spokesmen like Henry Wallace conducted a long campaign to educate Americans to a fundamental choice: a choice between a high-tariff policy which would convert the United States into a hermit nation of chronic rural depression, and a liberal commercial policy which would give it a balanced economy and a higher standard of living. Franklin D. Roosevelt was antagonistic to the Smoot–Hawley folly. He supported Secretary Hull in the latter's admirable reciprocal trade treaties, which achieved an unexpected success. The Roosevelt Administration thus adopted a policy which at last harmonizes with the American tradition of support for freedom of commerce and trade. There is ground for hope that it will cleave to this line.

Altogether, American foreign policy, like that of other nations, is a strand of many vari-coloured threads. Much of it has been opportunistic. Some of it has been selfish, and more of it blundering. But it has nevertheless been actuated by rather more of principle than the foreign policy of most lands. Of all the guiding traditions which we have named, that first described, adherence to democratic ideals, is by far the most important. It is the bedrock foundation of American action in foreign affairs. In times of crisis it always conditions the course of the Government. The great question is whether the tradition will be boldly or timidly sustained. Those who exaggerate the importance of avoiding foreign entanglements, and who mistake isolation for safety, stand for a timid adherence. But more than once the country has proved that when the need really arises, it will take the bold course. Remembering Jefferson's Declaration and Lincoln's Gettysburg speech, it will accept Woodrow Wilson's assertion that the world must be made safe for democracy, and Franklin D. Roosevelt's declaration that the democratic way of life must be defended whenever it is vitally endangered.

WORKING MEN'S
COLLEGE
LIBRARY

CHAPTER II

MEN AND CONTROLS

IT is sometimes said that the management of American foreign relations is to an exceptional degree irresponsible. Is it not affected by an emotional public opinion, by Press vagaries, and by politicians who play up to the galleries? Are not Presidents inclined to write rhetorical notes with an eye on the next election? Does foreign policy not veer with every change of Administration? To all these queries the answer is No. The management of foreign affairs may be highly informal; it may be marked by what John Hay called a "limpid simplicity" and may sometimes justify the term "shirt-sleeve" diplomacy, first used in 1895. But American public opinion is as responsible as that of any land. The most influential newspapers are sober and judicious. Foreign relations are fairly well insulated from the baser type of politics, and Presidents and Secretaries of State treat them, in general, with caution and high seriousness.

Under the Constitution, relations with other countries are managed exclusively by the Federal Government. The States are strictly forbidden to enter into any treaty, agreement, or compact with foreign nations. But the Constitution does not explicitly declare by what Federal agency external affairs are to be conducted. Apparently the fathers of the republic intended that the responsibility should be divided between the President and Senate. They ordained that the President "shall have power, by and with the advice and consent of the Senate, to make treaties, provided two-thirds of the Senators present concur". They also stipulated that the President "shall nominate, and by and with the advice of the Senate, shall appoint ambassadors, other public ministers, and consuls. . . ." Finally, it was provided that the President shall receive foreign envoys.

It thus appears that the authors of the Constitution intended to make the Senate a council on foreign affairs, working in collaboration with the President. But in actual practice, foreign affairs are primarily in the hands of the

President and the Secretary of State, an officer who is not named or explicitly provided for in the original Constitution. Above all, it is the President who usually formulates lines of action. He may announce them to Congress in a message, as Monroe did with his Doctrine, and Cleveland with his plan for marking the Venezuelan boundary. He may define them in a public speech, as Coolidge did when he turned his back on the World Court; or in a statement to the Press, as Wilson in 1913 announced his condemnation of dollar diplomacy; or in fireside chats to the nation, after the style of Franklin D. Roosevelt. He may even formulate them in a letter to an associate: Theodore Roosevelt made his first statement of his corollary to the Monroe Doctrine in a letter to Secretary Elihu Root, read at a New York banquet in the spring of 1904. But up to a certain line, the President always has power to make his own foreign policies.

That line is drawn in part by public opinion, as expressed by various organized groups, the Press, the radio, and public mass-meetings. Sometimes public opinion can push a President down a road that he is reluctant to take. McKinley in 1898 wished to avoid war with Spain. But a great part of the American electorate, aroused by the inhumanity of the war in Cuba, and excited by a sensational Press, prodded President and Congress into action. Sometimes a display of public opinion can block what seems a reasonable and even non-controversial policy of a President. The activities of highly organized pressure-groups, led by the Hearst newspapers and Father Coughlin, thus defeated the efforts of Franklin D. Roosevelt to carry the nation into the World Court. Of course it is difficult to say just what public opinion is on a given subject, and many problems in foreign affairs possess technical aspects which are not easily understood by the masses. But even the boldest President always takes account of general sentiment.

One group which manifests a considerable interest in foreign affairs is labour. The American Federation of Labour, through its Legislative Committee, a permanent body with headquarters in Washington, has exerted not a little influence. The head of this committee is always the President of the Federation, first Samuel Gompers, and then William Green. The A. F. of L. has at various times supported American participation in the World Court; the re-

striction of immigration; an early termination of Caribbean
intervention; and the limitation of armaments. It has stood
for Philippine independence—partly to stop the easy immigration of Filipino labour. In Mexican affairs it has steadily
supported such champions of the workers as Obregon and
Calles, and tended to discourage meddling from Washington.
The A. F. of L. voted in 1933 to boycott German goods and
services "until the German Government recognizes the
rights of the working-people of Germany to organize into
bona fide, independent trade unions of their own choosing
and until Germany ceases its repressive policy of persecution
of Jewish people". In general, the Federation has been
strongly opposed to fascism wherever it has appeared. In
1935 it voted concurrence with the League in declaring
Italy an outlaw nation, while in 1940 it came out strongly
for full aid to Great Britain. It must be reckoned a force on
the liberal side in matters of foreign policy.

The churches have usually treated foreign affairs with
caution, taking a definite stand only for idealistic and
pacifistic objects. Most Protestant sects gave their adherence
to the League cause in 1919–20, and to the World Court
later. Their general bias has been towards internationalism.
The Catholic Church was much chillier towards the League
and the World Court, primarily because of its many Irish-
American and German–American followers. When the
Mexican Government was conducting its bitter battle with
the hierarchy, the Catholics of the United States gave
numerous evidences of antagonism to the new regime.
Many Catholics during the civil war in Spain likewise
pressed for an arms embargo applicable to the Madrid
Government; but on this point the Church showed a
division. It is not unfair to call the Catholic Church predominantly isolationist.

Unquestionably the newspaper Press formerly exercised
a much larger influence over opinion on foreign affairs than
today. It was sometimes a decidedly pernicious influence.
The jingo chorus when Cleveland threatened Great Britain
over the Venezuela boundary, and when McKinley hesitated to go to war with Spain, was sickening. It justified the
solemn warnings which Lord Bryce had uttered against the
dangers that attended the rise of a sensational body of newspapers in a great democracy of newspaper-readers. Later

the excesses of the anti-Japanese newspapers on the Pacific Coast, particularly in 1905-7; the blatant Anglophobia of numerous journals when Congress was debating the repeal of the Panama Canal Tolls Act in 1913; and the attempt of the Hearst Press to whip up public feeling against Mexico during and after the World War, were most deplorable. But the Press has become more sober, moderate, and responsible. The rise of the cinema and radio, moreover, has deprived it of much of its old hold on the public mind. In general, the Press of the eastern seaboard is internationalist in temper, and great journals like the New York *Times* and *Herald-Tribune*, the Springfield *Republican*, and the Philadelphia *Record* are anxious that the United States should play its full part in world affairs, and play it creditably. The Middle West contains two strong isolationist organs, the St. Louis *Post-Dispatch* and the Chicago *Tribune;* but there are important journals on the other side, led by the Chicago *Daily News* and the St. Louis *Globe-Democrat.* The Southern Press is strongly tinctured by the ideas of Wilson and Franklin D. Roosevelt, and by the traditional Anglophile feeling of the section.

According to the census of 1930, the United States contained 13,366,407 persons of foreign birth. Of these the largest single group, the Italians, numbered 1,790,000; the next largest, the Germans, 1,608,000; the emigrants from Great Britain and Northern Ireland 1,402,000; the Canadians 1,278,000; and the Poles 1,268,000. Those born in what is now Eire came far to the rear, with only 745,000. A large proportion of the Canadians were of course French-Canadians. Beyond these foreign-born lay a still larger body of people whose parents or grandparents were foreign-born, and who felt some tie with the ancient motherland. Certain of the racial groups have not hesitated to take an active part in American politics. Irish-American organizations and German-American organizations were long especially prominent—and of course especially vociferous in foreign affairs. The deplorable activities of Daniel Cohalan and George Sylvester Viereck in World War days are still remembered, and on one famous occasion President Wilson refused to make a speech until the former had left the platform.

That Irish-American and German-American activities

long had an unhappy effect on American foreign relations nobody can doubt. Some leaders, like James G. Blaine, were all too ready to truckle to Irish-American voters by twisting the lion's tail. The wretched "Murchison letter" affair in 1888, when Sir Lionel Sackville-West, the British Minister in Washington, was tricked into writing a letter on American politics which caused the President to ask for his recall, was a direct product of the Republican desire to gain Irish-American votes. Olney's bellicose handling of the Venezuelan boundary dispute was received with a roar of applause by men of German and Irish blood. In 1900 John Hay, who had been promoting the Open Door policy, wrote to a friend: "That we should be compelled to refuse the assistance of the greatest power in the world, in carrying out our own policy, because all Irishmen are Democrats and some Germans are fools, is enough to drive a man mad." A North-western Senator said in 1914 that hardly a political campaign in any State "is not shaped to meet the special sentiments of this and that hyphenated element of our own country".

Both in making peace at Paris in 1919, and in his fight for the League afterwards, Wilson found hyphenated groups a source of endless trouble. The Italian-Americans strongly supported their motherland in demanding a Tyrolese frontier that included the Brenner Pass. They strongly resented Wilson's course with regard to Fiume. Senator Lodge asserted that this port was as essential to Italian welfare as was the possession of New Orleans to the United States; and when Henry White showed that it was really essential to Yugo-Slavia, not Italy, he remained unmoved. Massachusetts had a host of Italian-American voters, but few Yugo-Slavs! The Irish-Americans were affronted because Wilson refused to press Great Britain for the erection of an Irish republic. When the question of the League came before the Senate, two prominent Republicans visited the British Ambassador. They told him that in employing Irish issues to weaken Wilson and the League, they would have to make vicious attacks upon Great Britain; but that he should take this in a Pickwickian sense, as mere political thunder. Irish, German, and Italian bitterness in 1919–20 had not a little to do with the ultimate defeat of the League. And a little later a Senator told Paul Scott Mowrer that the United States could

III. SOME MAKERS OF AMERICAN FOREIGN POLICY

1. JAMES MONROE
(Brown Brothers, N.Y.)

2. THEODORE ROOSEVELT
(General Photographic Agency)

3. WOODROW WILSON
(Exclusive News Agency)

hardly take an active interest in European affairs, for nearly every question would arouse some hyphenated element. Washington, he thought, should concern itself with Japan, which controlled no votes!

All this was highly deplorable. But certain ameliorating considerations should be noted. First, some hyphenated elements often tended to cancel each other out. The British-born and many Canadian-born took a view directly opposed to that of the Irish-born; the Italian-born or Polish-born were likely to disagree with the German-born. Second, the World War had the effect of making "hyphenate" feeling unpopular and definitely eliminating much of it. During 1917–18 a host of Americans of German lineage shouldered arms against the Kaiser, and when the conflict ended were as staunchly American as the descendents of the Puritans. Third, the natural workings of the melting-pot, the process of Americanization, has made for a steady decay of foreign-language newspapers, magazines, and institutions. Most children of immigrants are ashamed of immigrant ways and speech. Intermarriage helps the pot to boil. And fourth, the immigration legislation which followed the World War has cut down the European inflow to a mere trickle, thus promoting assimilation. Under the law of 1924, not more than 150,000 aliens may be admitted in any year, apportioned by the percentage of each nationality resident in the United States in 1920. The overwhelming mass of the population are Americans, and neither less nor more.

Pressure-groups have always been and doubtless always will be a factor in foreign affairs. They range from loose combinations of munitions manufacturers to pacifist organizations, from the Daughters of the American Revolution to radical youth societies. But their power has been limited by two developments. In the first place, sociologists and political scientists have given the methods of the most troublesome pressure-groups expert study, and their techniques have been competently exposed. In the second place, the highly efficient polls devised in recent years (notably the Gallup and *Fortune* polls) have furnished a realistic gauge of public sentiment, and have served to deflate the claims of some minority groups. Test after test has vindicated the general accuracy of the Gallup and *Fortune* canvasses. In simple issues, where readily understandable questions can be phrased, they show just how the wind is bearing. And by doing this, they demonstrate that bodies which claim to represent tens of millions may actually be as insignificant as the tailors of Tooley Street.

If public opinion does much to limit the President's control of foreign relations, so does Congress. It can at any time intervene in the field, and frequently does. House and Senate are always free to pass resolutions calling upon the Chief Executive to take some specific step. In 1896, for example, they overwhelmingly voted a resolution calling for recognition of the belligerency of the Cuban insurgents; but Cleveland calmly ignored it. Senator Borah's resolution in 1921 for the calling of a tri-power disarmament conference was passed by Senate and House despite President Harding's covert opposition; and it brought about the Washington Conference later that year. Only the vigorous opposition of President Wilson in 1916 defeated the McLemore resolution calling upon him to warn American citizens not to travel on armed British merchant vessels. Sometimes Congress has gone quite beyond permissible bounds in interfering with the President's powers. It passed in 1913 an amendment to an appropriation bill which forbade the Chief Executive to offer or accept any invitation to participate "in any international congress, conference, or like event" without first receiving authority of law. Needless to say, Presidents have ignored this legislation, assuming it to be unconstitutional.

Congress is also free to pass resolutions condemning some act of a foreign nation, or requesting that nation to take a definite course. It thus assailed the treatment of the Jews by Tsarist Russia. In 1916 the Senate called upon the British Government to extend mercy to Sir Roger Casement, ordering that the resolution should be presented to the Foreign Office. Three years later the Senate voted an expression of its sympathy with the "aspirations of the Irish people for a government of their own choice", and added that when that Government was set up, "a consummation it is hoped is at hand", it should be admitted to the League. Happily, the British people and Government took this admonition good-naturedly. The political motive behind it, the desire of Senators to win Irish-American votes, was transparent; but it should also be said that it did represent a genuine feeling on the part of many old-stock Americans. The Senate and

House committees on foreign affairs, and indeed other committees, can hold hearings and issue reports which exert a wide influence. The Nye Committee on the munitions business is a striking example. Members of Congress can also take informal action, as thirty-nine Senators and Senators-elect did when they signed Lodge's round-robin asserting that the League in the form proposed to the peace conference should not be accepted by the United States.

But, above all, the Senate possesses the power to defeat any Presidential policy that is embodied in a treaty—and has often done so. One-third of that body, in which Western States of small population have precisely the same representation as crowded New York and Pennsylvania, can block all action. That is, an unrepresentative minority may destroy a treaty which the overwhelming majority of the American people strongly desire. It is far from impossible that a group of wilful Senators may be actuated in this, as John Hay once wrote, by "personal interest, personal spites, and a contingent chance of petty political advantage". In the period 1897–1921 the Senate seemed prone to take an increasingly arrogant advantage of its special position. Hay spoke for some of his successors when he remarked that in dealing with foreign nations he felt as if he had one hand tied behind his back, and a ball and chain on his leg.

President Grant never forgave the Senate for rejecting his treaty for the annexation of Santo Domingo. Presidents Cleveland and McKinley were deeply grieved by the defeat in 1897 of the arbitration treaty with Great Britain which they, and enlightened sentiment throughout America, hoped would be approved. John Hay was so despondent over the defeat of the first Hay-Pauncefote treaty regarding an isthmian canal that he contemplated resignation, and predicted that no important treaty would ever again pass the Senate. But this defeat, like that of the Santo Domingo treaty, was really for the national good, and a better compact was soon ratified. When the Democratic party lost control of the Senate in the elections of 1918, ex-President Roosevelt hastened to assure the globe that President Wilson was left without authority in foreign relations. "His leadership has just been emphatically repudiated. . . . The newly-elected Congress comes far nearer than Mr. Wilson to having the right to speak for the purposes of the American people at this moment." The Treaty of Versailles, fiercely contested as soon as it entered the Senate, was finally defeated. There can be little doubt that majority sentiment was heavily behind Wilson, but it was impossible to obtain a two-thirds vote.

Even when a treaty is ratified, the Senate may attach crippling stipulations. One expert on government, J. W. Garner, wrote in 1927 that in recent years the Senate had shown "almost a mania for amending treaties or giving its advice and consent subject to reservations and conditions". This has been especially true of multilateral treaties. To the Four-Power Treaty of 1922 the Senate tacked one of its inevitable reservations: "there is no commitment to armed force, no alliance, no obligation to join in any defense". All plans for the adherence of the United States to the World Court have been done to death by Senate reservations pushed to a preposterous extreme.

Inevitably, the great power lodged in a Senate minority, and in the Senate Committee on Foreign Relations, has been the target of much denunciation. This has been especially true since 1918, for the Senate's authority has been an issue in the bitter struggle between internationalists and isolationists. Garner called the existing requirement an undemocratic feature which has "led to devastating results". Ray Stannard Baker asserted that it caused "utter weakness, muddle, and delay", and that "it not only disgraces us before the nations, but in some future world crisis may ruin us". George W. Wickersham termed the treaty-making machinery of the republic "so complicated as to be almost unworkable", and thought that until the system was changed, only a widespread and forcible expression of public opinion could bring the United States into helpful co-operation with other nations. The Senate has had its defenders, who point out that most treaties have been accepted and that delay has sometimes been valuable. But the criticism is nevertheless valid. No other important nation, not even in Latin America, gives a minority in one chamber so much power over treaties. Only the intense political conservatism of the American people, and the difficulty of amending the Constitution, have prevented a long-overdue change.

The President proposes; the Senate disposes—so it might often be written in our history. While the Chief Executive can chart a course, the winds of Congressional antagonism may completely wreck his plans. Other governments must always take account of this uncertainty. It is conceivable that under certain circumstances they might take advantage of it. In 1918 Henry Cabot Lodge sent to Henry White, of the peace delegation in Paris, a memorandum which he asked White to show to some of Wilson's opponents abroad in order to strengthen them against the President. This base attempt to undermine Wilson's position failed, for White never considered showing the document to any European diplomat. But it had its significant implications.

It is because of the Senate's exaggerated powers to maim, delay, or defeat a treaty that able and resolute Presidents have often presented Congress with a *fait accompli*, which it must willy-nilly accept; that they have taken their policy around the Senate rather than through its doors. John Hay in 1899 committed the United States to the Open Door in China, and did a good deal to commit other Powers, without ever consulting Congress. Theodore Roosevelt encouraged the revolt in Panama in 1903, and came near conniving at it; his prompt recognition of the new Panama Republic committed the United States to the dismemberment of Colombia; and he then received a handpicked envoy from Panama (actually a French citizen) with whom he negotiated a treaty so advantageous to the United States that the Senate could not reject it. His "cowboy diplomacy" was branded by the Springfield *Republican* as one of the most disgraceful incidents in American history, and by the New York *Nation* as buccaneering; but it succeeded. Equally imperious was Franklin D. Roosevelt's transfer of fifty destroyers to Britain in 1940 without a word to Congress.

Nor is the President always helpless even when he has been flatly rebuffed by the Senate. John Tyler in 1844 laid before the upper chamber a treaty for the annexation of Texas. He was distressed but not daunted when it failed to secure the necessary two-thirds majority. As it was impossible to overcome the hostile minority, he turned to another course. A joint resolution could be passed by majority vote in both houses, and Tyler effected annexation by joint resolution. Critics who denied the constitutionality of this method were brusquely overruled. When Theodore Roosevelt decided to send the fleet around the world in 1907, he met strong opposition, and the chairman of the Senate Naval Affairs Committee told him that no money would be appropriated for the harebrained adventure. Roosevelt rejoined that he had money enough on hand to send the fleet into the Pacific, and that it could stay there if the Senate did not wish to bring it back. In 1917, again, Wilson attempted to induce Congress to vote for the arming of American merchantmen against German submarines. He was defeated by "a little group of wilful men" who at the close of the session arranged a filibuster.[1] Thereupon he cut the Gordian knot by issuing an executive order, as commander-in-chief, for the arming of the vessels.

And a President can reach important agreements of his own, so long as they are not too formal and far-reaching, with foreign nations. In 1907 relations between the United States and Japan were badly strained by the hostility of the Californians to Japanese immigrants. Theodore Roosevelt temporarily ended the difficulty by the Gentlemen's Agreement with Japan, which was embodied in a series of diplomatic notes. Its full terms were not even revealed. A decade later American-Japanese relations had again become troubled, this time by friction in China. Viscount Ishii went to Washington, and held a series of conversations with the Secretary of State. The result was the Lansing–Ishii Agreement, again embodied in a series of notes. It was fiercely attacked in the United States as surrendering important American interests in China, but the Senate was given no opportunity whatever to vote on it. Again, the great deal by which Franklin D. Roosevelt took over from Great Britain in 1940 a string of sites for bases was not submitted to the Senate.

It will be seen that the most rigid feature in the control of American foreign relations is the constitutional provision that two-thirds of the Senate must ratify any treaty. It is altogether too rigid, and may well in time be changed. All else is healthfully fluid, uncontrolled by any long array of rules and dogmas. The President can appoint personal agents to aid him in his diplomacy, as Polk chose Nicholas Trist, and Woodrow Wilson used Colonel House. He can go to almost any length so long as he is clearly supported by public opinion, plays his cards well, and is not too unlucky

[1] A prolonged, irrelevant speech to defeat a bill on time.

with obstructionists in the Senate. If he acts in the face of public opinion, he will not get far. Even the House of Representatives, which nominally has no voice in foreign affairs, may sometimes thwart him by the simple expedient of refusing to pass needed appropriations.

But what of the Department of State, of the men who have filled it, and of their relations to President and Senate? The Secretary of State fills a double rôle. He is adviser to the President, to the Senate Committee on Foreign Relations, and to inquiring Congressmen; he is also head of a huge and busy department which embraces all ambassadors, ministers, special envoys, and consuls, and which handles an immense body of routine diplomatic and commercial business. The department has to deal with shipping, tariffs, trade promotion, and all the troubles and complaints of citizens abroad. Among its numerous divisions are one on research and publication, one on the Philippines, one on international conferences, and one on cultural relations. It trains young men for foreign service and advances them systematically to posts of increasing responsibility. The Secretary by no means spends all his time interpreting the Monroe Doctrine, handling League relations, and dealing with European crises. He spends much of it seeing that his administrative machine, so important to American economic interests, moves smoothly and effectively.

The roster of Secretaries from Thomas Jefferson in 1790 to Cordell Hull in 1941 is long. It includes some men who achieved their principal distinction in other offices. Among them are Jefferson, Madison, Monroe, John Quincy Adams, and Van Buren, who became Presidents; Calhoun, Webster, and Blaine, who were great parliamentary leaders; and John Marshall and Charles E. Hughes, known primarily as jurists. It includes, of course, a number of nonentities. But by common consent five Secretaries represent genuine eminence in the conduct of foreign relations—an eminence comparable to that of the best British Foreign Ministers— John Quincy Adams, Daniel Webster, Hamilton Fish, John Hay, and Cordell Hull.

The relations between Presidents and Secretaries of State vary with times and temperaments. Sometimes the President has decidedly taken the reins into his own control. One of the dramatic moments in the early history of the republic vas that, in 1798, when John Adams, seeing that Secretary Pickering was headed straight for war with France, suddenly ook over foreign affairs and sharply changed the course of the Government. Of the Presidents who followed him, Jefferson made his own foreign policy with only slight attention to Secretary Madison—though the two were in natural agreement. Andrew Jackson steered his own course. James K. Polk's diary shows that he entered the presidency with clearly-defined objects in the foreign as well as in the domestic sphere, and that his shrewd, stubborn, dogmatic mind insisted on gaining them.

In more recent times, Theodore Roosevelt greatly enjoyed foreign affairs, and gave them exuberant attention. This was not always to the public benefit, for he was an exponent of vigorous, hard-hitting methods. Elihu Root, when Roosevelt protested once in a Cabinet meeting that he had good grounds for taking Panama, sarcastically remarked 'Oh, Mr. President, do not let any taint of legality mar the boldness of that exploit!' First Hay and then Root spent much time in repressing Roosevelt's more erratic impulses and in giving his acts a veneer of courtesy that he was prone to neglect. But it was by Roosevelt's will that Panama was made nominally independent in 1903; that the Alaskan boundary dispute was "adjudicated" under something close to American duress; and that the Big Stick was waved in Morocco (just before the Republican Convention of 1904) to save a supposed American citizen who was really, as Roosevelt knew, a Greek subject. Roosevelt took great pride in his rôle in 1905 as peacemaker between Russia and Japan, and in 1906 in the Algeçiras Conference. He wrote to a friend that, in the latter affair, he treated the Kaiser courteously, 'yet when it became necessary at the end I stood him on his head with great decision".

In a more critical period, Woodrow Wilson was his own Secretary of State. To be sure, Secretary Bryan was allowed to carry through his "cooling-off" treaties of conciliation pacts with thirty nations. But in all important matters Wilson developed his own policies. Indeed, a close student (Harley Notter in *The Origins of the Foreign Policy of Woodrow Wilson*) holds that all his essential ideas in the international field were fixed before he entered the White House. He refused at first to encourage the Wall Street bankers in

China and Latin America; but later he did produce his own brand of dollar diplomacy. He insisted upon repeal of a dishonourable law which had excepted American coastwise shipping from the payment of Panama Canal tolls. He pursued his own highly moralistic line in the Mexican tangle. Some observers, when he refused to recognize Huerta, asked what right an American President had to say who should be President of Mexico. But Wilson felt no doubts. "I am going to teach the Latin American republics to elect good men!" he told Sir William Tyrrell.

Wilson took that unyielding stand in defence of freedom of the seas which did so much to bring the United States into war with Germany. He himself, sitting down to his battered typewriter, wrote the eloquent notes of protest which the American Government sent to Berlin. When he drafted his second note on the *Lusitania*, William Jennings Bryan resigned on the ground that it was leading to hostilities. The new Secretary of State, Robert Lansing, was little more than Wilson's diplomatic clerk. It was Wilson alone (though counselled by Colonel House) who decided upon the final agonized effort in 1916 to bring the world back to peace; who broke with Germany when Berlin resumed unrestricted submarine warfare; and who, after painful hesitation in April, 1917, asked Congress for war with Germany. At Paris, later, Wilson took all too little advice from Lansing and his other associates.

Yet not infrequently a strong Secretary has been given a fairly free hand. This happens when a President is immersed in home problems, knows that he is grossly ignorant of foreign affairs, or feels overawed by an especially able Secretary.

The voluminous diary of John Quincy Adams shows that he managed foreign affairs under President Monroe (a much weaker man) with little interference. He had delicate and important problems to solve. They included recognition of the new Latin-American republics, the acquisition of Florida, and the settlement of difficulties with Britain left by the War of 1812. A man of hard-headed power, Adams dealt with them in a masterful way. Daniel Webster enjoyed a similar freedom in 1841–43 in settling the vexatious boundary between Maine and Canada, with certain other differences between Britain and America. President Tyler was absorbed at the moment in internal affairs. In any event, he would have deferred to Webster's intellectual power, ripe experience, and force of personality. By judicious negotiations with Lord Ashburton, a fair compromise was devised. Not only was a troublesome issue thus settled, but a spirit was created between the two English-speaking Powers which conduced to a friendly settlement of other questions down to 1860. Later, in Taylor's brief administration, Webster again managed the State Department with a vigorous hand.

A striking instance of State Department autonomy can be found in the Grant Administration. The President was frankly ignorant of alien lands, and blundered whenever he touched foreign relations. Secretary Fish was one of the most astute, industrious, and cultivated of all those who have held the office. It fell to him to deal with several grave Anglo-American controversies, chief among them the dispute over the damage wrought by the British-built *Alabama* and other Confederate cruisers. By the Treaty of Washington, he arranged the first great international arbitration of modern times. It also fell to Fish to manage Spanish relations when Cuba was in revolt and powerful American groups were demanding intervention. He resisted all the jingoist pressure and kept the peace. In other important matters the Secretary maintained a firm grasp.

But in general, foreign affairs are best managed by a constant collaboration between President and Secretary of State. A President normally knows much more about public sentiment than any Cabinet member. A Secretary normally knows much more about what is occurring abroad than the busy President can learn. Even the strongest President needs technical advice on international law and diplomatic procedure; even the ablest Secretary needs a President's advice and support. In most Administrations foreign affairs have been managed by the two men working together. Frequently they have made a strong pair. Adams and Clay, Tyler and Calhoun, Cleveland and Bayard, McKinley and Hay, Hoover and Stimson, all were excellent teams. So, after an initial trial of strength, were Lincoln and Seward. Really vital questions of policy are likely to come before the whole Cabinet, with Administration leaders in Congress called in. One-man management will be increasingly rare.

A good impression of the way foreign problems have been thrashed out under Franklin D. Roosevelt is given in Alsop and Kinter's *American White Paper*. It describes frequent conferences in which Roosevelt, Secretary Hull, Under-Secretary Sumner Welles, and Assistant-Secretary Adolf A. Berle participated. Sometimes these occurred in the executive offices, sometimes in the President's comfortable upstairs study, sometimes early in the morning in his bedroom. In the State Department itself another set of conferences would meet, including J. P. Moffat and J. C. Dunn, who preside over the Western European division, with perhaps other higher officials. The President knew about these State Department gatherings. If one seemed especially important, he would summon Hull and Welles to talk with him in advance, and deliver his opinion to guide the deliberations of the Department. Roosevelt has kept in touch with the principal ambassadors in Europe by trans-Atlantic telephone. Alsop and Kintner tell us how important notes were written. "When he has other men draft for him, the President habitually gives them a detailed outline of what he wants, noting the points to be covered, describing the tone to be taken, and specifying the length of the draft. Often he also supplies the key phrase or paragraph." Frequently drafts would be revised again and again. At the time of the Italian march into Albania, Roosevelt took nearly a week, with numerous conferences, to produce his remarkable note to Hitler and Mussolini.

The State Department, long ill-officered and neglected, has in the last generation become much more expertly staffed. In Fish's day it was badly housed in an old orphan asylum; its few clerks, jammed into tiny rooms, were heavily overtasked. Down to 1900 all important posts were filled on the spoils system, so that nearly a clean sweep might occur every four years. For almost a century two men, and two alone, gave the Department what continuity it possessed. William Hunter entered it in 1829, serving for fifty-seven years, and becoming Second Assistant-Secretary of State. Before he left, A. A. Adee entered in 1879, and remaining for forty-seven years, attained the same rank. Both were invaluable. They became so versed in precedent and international law that they could prevent the most persistently amateurish Secretary from making blunders; and they gave

American policy a degree of consistency that it would otherwise have lacked. For thirty years Adee—deaf, shrewd, witty, and alert—passed on practically all the communications which went out of the State Department, and wrote thousands of them himself.

Since World War days the department has become as highly organized as any foreign office in the world. It has divisions devoted to the American republics, to European affairs, to Near Eastern affairs, and to Far Eastern affairs. It has a counsellor chosen for proficiency in international law, and a legal adviser. Besides the Under-Secretary (now Sumner Welles) and the two Assistant-Secretaries (now Adolf A. Berle and Breckinridge Long), it has several special assistants, three advisers on political relations, and one adviser on economic affairs. A special officer looks after foreign service administration, another after foreign service personnel, and a third after the foreign service officers' training school. There are numerous other divisions. Records are cared for by the bureau of indexes and archives and the historical adviser. To the department flows information from all parts of the globe. President Hoover said in 1929 that it "must be supported and strengthened as the great arm of our government dedicated to peace", and appropriations have not been stinted.

The diplomatic service has also become more expert and professional. During the nineteenth century appointments were primarily political, though a happy leavening of authors was provided. The service did better work than might have been expected. Not infrequently the more conspicuous posts (London, Paris, Berlin, and, towards the end of the century, Tokyo, Rio de Janeiro, and Buenos Aires) were filled by men of eminence. To be sure, such a man as Robert C. Schenck became Minister to England, and disgraced it by promoting a speculative mining property. But England also received such fine figures as James Russell Lowell, Charles Francis Adams, Thomas F. Bayard, Whitelaw Reid, and John Hay. Some sorry party hacks were sent to Paris and Berlin. But so were men of brains like John Bigelow, Andrew D. White, and William E. Dodd. No better diplomatists could have been found than Anson Burlingame and Dwight Morrow, sent to China and Mexico respectively.

D (N.)

It was chiefly in the lesser posts that the spoils system gave
the United States a poor representation. When Fish laid
before Grant clear evidence that some of the men he was
appointing were disgracefully unfit, Grant imperturbably
replied: "Well, it is a good thing to get such fellows out of
the country." Hay spoke of the Presidential habit of raking
the list of Keeley cures (for habitual drunkards) to fill minor
ministerial posts.

Today it is precisely the lesser offices which have been pro-
fessionalized. In 1906 the consular service was brought
under civil service rules, to its immediate benefit; and three
years later the same rules were applied to the lower grades
of the diplomatic service. Then in 1924 the Rogers Act
merged the two branches into one, the United States
Foreign Service; a classified service, entered by examina-
tion, in which promotion from stage to stage is won by
merit. Members may be moved to duty in the consular
or diplomatic division, as the President orders, and are
expected to know much of both. In theory the President
and Senate may appoint men to either service as before,
but in fact the choice is increasingly made not from
amateurs, but from career men—*i.e.*, professional diplomats trained in the permanent civil service. The first true
"career diplomatist" was Henry White, in succession First
Secretary of the London embassy, Ambassador to Italy and
France, and a member of Wilson's Peace Commission.

But the highest posts, being connected with government
policy, are still filled chiefly by political appointees. The
theory is that ambassadors to the greatest nations should be
men of wide business and political experience, and of independent fortune. Actually many of the men chosen are
mediocre politicians, campaign-donors, or journalists whose
service to the party demands a recompense. Others may be
leaders of eminence and ability. The present administration
offers examples of both types. Mr. Winant, a life-long
Republican, was obviously made Ambassador to Great
Britain because of his ability, experience, and breadth of
vision. Other ambassadors could be named who were
selected because they had money, social position, and a
record of cheerful giving to party chests. Yet to an increasing
extent the secondary as well as tertiary posts are filled by
professional diplomats. Hugh Gibson, William C. Grew,

Norman H. Davis, and Hugh Wilson are among those who thus served the country in important posts for many years.

Americans of isolationist stamp like to depreciate the ability of the State Department and diplomatic corps. They propagate the view that the men charged with our foreign relations are mere children compared with the astute, sophisticated, and tricky European leaders. The facts do not support this tendentious attitude. No nation has produced an abler list of foreign ministers than Adams, Webster, Seward, Fish, Hay, and Hull. None has produced abler ambassadors than the best men in the long roster from Benjamin Franklin onwards. The weakest American agents have never made such blunders as some British and European diplomats have made in America.

Nor is the record of the United States in foreign affairs that of a nation constantly overreached by sharper traders. On the contrary, in a long series of transactions—the settlement of the Maine boundary, the Oregon boundary, the Alaskan boundary; the adjustment of the *Alabama* claims by a handsome indemnity; the settlement of the Newfoundland fisheries question; the abrogation of the Hay-Pauncefote treaty; the tripartite Samoan arrangement—the United States emerged from the negotiations with a distinct advantage. In the eyes of the outside world, American foreign relations have often been managed blatantly, with altogether too much emphasis on the ideas of "America first" and "My country, right or wrong"—which Carl Schurz said was equivalent to "My mother, drunk or sober." They have often been managed unctuously, in the spirit of Senator Beveridge's remark in imperialist days that God has " marked us as His chosen people, henceforth to lead in the regeneration of the world". They have sometimes been managed hypocritically, with a feeling that somehow America's hasty recognition of Panama was virtuous, while Japan's hasty recognition of Manchukuo was wicked. But in the eyes of the outside world, America has never managed her foreign affairs incompetently or with inadequate attention to self-interest. A glance at the map and a reference to the history of her territorial acquisitions will dispel the idea that the United States has been an abused international waif.

The gravest fault of American policy has been a recent

lack of strength in matters of world interest as distinguished from national interest. Between 1921 and 1937 it failed to behave as the wealthiest nation on the planet, the principal exporting nation, the chief financial power, and the strongest industrial country, ought to have behaved.

WORKING MEN'S COLLEGE LIBRARY

CHAPTER III

HISTORICALLY, America's most important external relations have been with the British Empire. Her longest land boundary is with Canada, and Canadian foreign policy until a generation ago was controlled from London. British sea-power has always been a primary factor in the American outlook. Sometimes it has injured the United States, as during the Napoleonic Wars; frequently it has been an irritant; but it has often been advantageous, as during the long decades when it was the principal bulwark of the Monroe Doctrine. America's commercial relations with the Empire have far transcended in importance those with any other Power. Of late years the people of the United States have felt a certain kinship with the young Dominions. And for good or ill the British attitude towards American ways, institutions, and policies has, because of the ties of blood, language, letters, law, and custom, meant a good deal to the republic, and affected its acts.

The direct foundations for a more cordial relation between America and Britain began to be laid at the turn of the last century. It would perhaps be more realistic to speak of the foundations for a diminution of hostility; for as late as 1895 relations could hardly have been worse. That was the year in which Great Britain's supposed encroachments upon Venezuela, where the boundary had long been unsettled, seemed to many Americans insufferable. Stiff and acrimonious notes were exchanged. Finally, Cleveland sent Congress a message in which he proposed that the United States should fix the true boundary, and intimated that if Britain crossed it she would be resisted by force. For a few days war seemed possible. But the lowering clouds rapidly blew away. For one reason, London consented to a limited arbitration; and for another, Cleveland's hasty message evoked from both sides of the Atlantic an astonishing manifestation of friendship.

This fervent expression of a conviction that the two English-speaking Powers must not quarrel, that any thought of war was intolerable, proved the most permanent result of the Venezuelan incident. Truculent voices were heard on both shores. But some of the most powerful American journals, led by Pulitzer's *World*, attacked Cleveland's action bitterly. Protests poured in upon Washington. The Protestant churches took a determined stand; business leaders in both lands, disturbed by a stock-market break, rose in dissent. Several hundred members of Parliament united in a cordial message to Congress. Altogether, the widespread condemnation of Salisbury's stubborn position in England, and of Cleveland's bellicose attitude in America, left the two countries in a more amicable mood than for years previously.

And this was but the beginning, for the next fifteen years brought about a striking Anglo-American *rapprochement*. Its primary basis was practical, not sentimental. The United States was annexing islands, building a canal, constructing a fleet, and becoming a true world Power; it realized that it needed British support. Great Britain was disturbed by the rise of Germany as a threatening rival in business, diplomacy, and armed might. It needed American amity, and Henry Adams has recorded his astonishment at the sudden purrings of the British lion to Americans. A number of steps, in conjunction with pre-existing forces, brought the two countries into highly cordial relations before the World War. In this way the whole future of the world was changed —for without this cordiality, Germany might never have been defeated in 1918.

(1) When the United States went to war with Spain in 1898, Great Britain displayed a sympathy all the more striking for its contrast with the hostility of most of Continental Europe. London bloomed with American flags, and the English rejoiced over Dewey's victory at Manila as an Anglo-Saxon triumph. That summer a German squadron in Manila Bay gave Dewey much anxiety, while the British squadron under Captain Edward Chichester furnished him with no little moral support. American feeling was also affected by the friendly attitude of most English journals in the next few years; by the pains taken to fill the Washington embassy with well-liked men—first Julian Pauncefote, then

IV. PAN-AMERICANISM

1 and 2. MEETINGS IN SESSION (*Wide World Photos*.)
3. PAN-AMERICAN BUILDING, WASHINGTON (*Wide World Photos*.)

WORKING MEN'S COLLEGE LIBRARY

James Bryce; and by the general British attention to hands across the sea, or cultural and social ties.

(2) Immediately after the Spanish War the United States and Great Britain formulated the Open-Door policy in China. The idea originated in London, and two Britons, Lord Charles Beresford and Arthur E. Hippisley, did much to convert Washington to it. Secretary Hay gave it final form, and pressed it upon the world. It harmonized with America's new imperialist policy in taking over the Philippines, a policy which Britain supported in other ways. Meanwhile, Britain remained a free trade country, increasingly open to American products, and friendly to commercial freedom everywhere.

(3) The British Government made a series of diplomatic concessions which contributed greatly to mutual goodwill. As the century opened it gave up very definite rights in Central America in order to grant the United States a free hand in building the Panama Canal. That is, it consented to the abrogation of the Clayton–Bulwer Treaty, which had provided that Britain and America were to have equal privileges in any isthmian canal, and that neither was to fortify it or enjoy exclusive rights over it. The generous Hay–Pauncefote treaty which gave this consent proved a milestone in the history of Anglo-American friendship. Shortly afterwards, Great Britain took a course in the Venezuelan debt question which again pleased the United States. To enforce certain claims against the unscrupulous dictator Castro, Britain, Germany, and Italy late in 1902 blockaded the Venezuelan coast, and the Germans sank two gunboats. But when Great Britain perceived that this was irritating to the United States, she consented to arbitration much more readily than the Kaiser. The American people contrasted the British attitude favourably with the "mailed-fist" tactics of the Germans, who had even bombarded a Venezuelan village.

Later still the British Government assisted in a disposition of the Canadian–Alaskan boundary issue which highly gratified Americans. The question was whether the disputed line of the Alaskan "panhandle" ran around the heads of certain inlets on the Pacific coast, as the United States asserted, or across the heads, as Canadians contended. The matter was referred to a panel of jurists representing Canada, the United States, and Great Britain. The British jurist, Lord Alverstone, consistently voted with the Americans and against the Canadians—as justice really demanded. It was a not unimportant demonstration of British fairness.

(4) The British navy was redistributed in 1906 in three fleets, the Mediterranean based on Malta, the Channel based on home ports, and the Atlantic based on Gibraltar. The squadron based on Bermuda to cover the Caribbean was recalled. This was primarily because of the German threat; but the United States, now building a really strong navy, appreciated the free hand given it in waters adjoining the canal.

All these events reinforced the ties long knit by blood, literature, law, and common ideals and traditions. And such bonds were further strengthened by another fact. American and British life and ways were steadily becoming more alike. As the United States became a crowded industrial democracy, it faced many of the problems of urban life, cyclical depression, and social unrest that the British had met much earlier. In dealing with these problems it drew heavily upon British experience. The measures of business control and social welfare undertaken by Theodore Roosevelt, Woodrow Wilson, and Franklin D. Roosevelt owed much to British precedent. At the same time, Great Britain was becoming socially and politically far more of a democracy than it had been during the nineteenth century. It drew heavily on the principles of democracy illustrated in America. This growing similarity between the two nations was comprehended subconsciously rather than explicitly, but it was none the less potent.

The World War, bringing the two nations into close partnership, was of course a solvent of many old-time misunderstandings, and a great cementing force. But after the struggle ended the new concord was marred by several factors. The war debt owed by Great Britain ($4,277,000,000 in principal alone) became a distinct irritant. Britons considered the American debt-settlement of 1923 a hard bargain. The criticisms expressed by Lloyd George and others did not please America. It was France and Belgium which, on December 15, 1932, led the procession of outright defaulters. But when the British Government followed suit in 1934, after a vain effort to maintain token payments, most Americans refused to discriminate among the defaulters. They realized that the debts were dead; and beyond question they felt disillusioned and resentful as they thought of the ten odd billions [1] loaned to Europe with all too little return. The default accentuated the isolationist spirit of these years. Meanwhile, Britons resented the failure of Americans to realize that they had paid off most of the *principal* of their debt.

Other irritants were furnished by economic competition in Latin America and China, by tariff barriers, and by the failure of the two Governments to achieve a common policy against Japan in 1931–33. Even during the World War many Americans had believed that Britain was making unfair use of the rigidly controlled shipping facilities to gain advantages in South American and Oriental trade. After the war, export rivalry became sharp. As for tariffs, the United States was chiefly to blame. The Fordney–McCumber and Smoot–Hawley tariffs aroused resentment throughout the globe. More than a score of nations retaliated against American goods; but it was the British reply in the Ottawa Agreements that was most stingingly effective. These commercial hostilities were unfortunate, for they sowed a crop of trade dislocation and ill-feeling. Of the failure of Stimson and Simon to act harmoniously in the Far East, more will be said on a later page.

But on the whole the gains effected earlier in the century were retained. At the Washington Conference in 1921 the British delegates, led by Balfour, accepted the American proposals with far more alacrity than did the French and Japanese—Americans fully appreciated the fact that Great Britain gave up the Anglo-Japanese alliance in part to please Canada, but more largely to satisfy the United States. They appreciated the fact also that the United States and Britain were still the main guarantors of the Open Door. The British release of Egypt and the British steps to give India fuller self-government quieted a great deal of criticism in America. But above all, the settlement between Ireland and Great Britain at almost one stroke destroyed the principal root of anti-British agitation—an agitation that had been incessant and embittered.

It was high time. The summer of 1920 witnessed numer-

[1] American billions (1,000,000,000).

ous mass meetings of Irish sympathizers in the larger
American cities; great processions were staged; and British
flags were torn from buildings. On St. Patrick's Day that year
army officers were forbidden to march in Irish demonstra-
tions. When the head of the Massachusetts branch of the
American Association for the Recognition of the Irish Republic demanded that Harding should revoke the order,
the President had to telegraph him that "the military and
naval forces of the nation can have no part in any demonstration which may be construed as influencing the foreign
relations of the republic." The New York *Nation* set on foot
an "investigation" which, though it may have been intended
to help Ireland, most certainly had the primary result of
arousing sentiment against Britain. But the establishment
of the Irish Free State, as independent as Canada or
Australia, assuaged the inveterate racial hatred. By 1940
the old Irish grievances were largely forgotten; the British
Government was given due credit for its generous course;
and Alfred E. Smith, most famous of Irish-Americans, for-
got his feud with Roosevelt in urging prompt, liberal, and
unceasing aid to Britain against the totalitarian states.

It was plain to Americans after the World War, as just
before it, that in most fields of foreign policy their central
aims harmonized with those of the British Empire; and more
than this, that in many ways Britain and America needed
each other's support. Washington and London were equally
interested in the protection of Canada. They were equally
interested in China's independence and integrity. The
United States would have been deeply disturbed by any
threat to Australia and New Zealand. Though Great
Britain and the United States were keen commercial rivals
in Latin America and the Orient, their competition, unlike
that which Germany offered to the United States, was based
on common economic assumptions. The United States insisted at the Washington Conference upon naval parity with
Great Britain, but even the admirals seldom talked in terms
of conflict. Instead, it was increasingly assumed that,
especially in the Pacific, the two navies would have to work
in harmony. And under all else lay the iron framework of
commercial interdependence. In 1937 the trade of the
United States (import and export combined) with Canada
amounted to £227 millions, and with the United Kingdom

to £185 millions, as against a total of £123 millions with Japan, and £60 millions with Germany.

Canada, especially, provided a powerful link between the two Powers. Intercourse between the Dominion and the Republic has been so free that the unfortified boundary line is in most respects almost invisible. Large numbers of American farmers have migrated to the prairie provinces, while a host of Eastern Canadians have moved into New England and the Middle Atlantic States. A reciprocity treaty pressed in 1911 by President Taft and Sir Wilfrid Laurier unfortunately failed because many Canadians regarded it as a first step towards annexation to the United States, while American farmers and lumbermen shrank from Dominion competition. But the Canadian and American economies have become to a great extent supplementary. While American industry is highly developed and diversified, Canada's remains primarily a processing industry, which prepares agricultural, mineral, and forest products for export, to be given final treatment elsewhere. Hull succeeded at an early date in signing a reciprocal trade treaty with Canada, which was renewed in 1938. A treaty for the development of the St. Lawrence Waterway was defeated by the American Senate in 1934, but this was merely a postponement. As Roosevelt said, it would yet go through "as sure as God made little apples".

The growing threat of the dictator states naturally served to bring the United States and Canada closer together. And when on August 18, 1938, Roosevelt made his dramatic statement at Kingston, Canada: "I give to you assurance that the people of the United States will not stand idly by if domination of Canadian soil is threatened by any other empire," this inclusion of the Dominion within the Monroe Doctrine was received with general applause. In her present position, Canada can be an invaluable interpreter of British ideas and aims to the United States, of American ideals and aims to Britain.

It would be impossible to exaggerate the value to America of her increasingly cordial relations with the British Commonwealth; relations that removed all anxiety on the very fronts which might have been most worrisome. They were dynamic relations. It was evident by 1925 to those who peered into the future that Canada and Australasia would

V. UNITED STATES BOUNDARIES

1 and 2. "THE UNDEFENDED FRONTIER",
CANADA–U.S.A.
(*Wide World Photos.*)

3. ON THE MEXICAN BORDER
(*Wide World Photos.*)

gravitate closer to the United States, while Britain would evince a growing willingness to admit that Washington, not London, is the foremost capital of the world. Only less important—indeed, only less indispensable—was the improvement in United States' relations with Latin America.

The reasons why Americans attach a special importance to their relations with Hispanic America are numerous and varied. The twenty southern republics cover an area about two and a half times as great as that of the United States, and already have a population of 125 millions. South America is one of the richest storehouses of raw materials on the globe; so rich, and yet so ill-developed, that it has been certain to attract the covetous eyes of Germany and Italy. Some of the Latin-American exports are necessities, or nearly that, to American economy: the coffee and rubber of Brazil, the coffee and petroleum of Colombia, the tin of Bolivia, the copper and nitrates of Chile, and the fruits of the "banana republics" in Central America. Before the World War, Great Britain was the principal source of capital to Latin America, but since 1918 the United States has been the chief investing nation. High hopes have been pinned to the development of Latin-American trade, and they have not been unjustified. Repeatedly, the value of American exports to South America alone has exceeded £125 millions, and once it passed £155 millions.

Politically, the United States has, of course, felt a special concern for the Latin American countries. During the early revolts against Spain it took a keen interest in what Henry Clay called "the glorious spectacle of eighteen millions of people, struggling to burst their chains and be free". Later it went to war for "Cuba Libre". All the republics have paid the United States the compliment of imitating the general outlines of its government. And since the promulgation of the Monroe Doctrine, Americans have painted a somewhat fanciful mental portrait of Uncle Sam as guardian of his southern neighbours.

To be sure, during the whole first century of the Monroe Doctrine its principal object and utility was to strengthen the security of the United States. It was often neglected when it did not serve that purpose. But the incidents which have most impressed the American imagination, such as the virtual expulsion of the French from Mexico after the Civil

War and Cleveland's defiance of Lord Salisbury, were those in which the nation, however mixed its motives, could pose as the benevolent ward of the weaker republics. These episodes in North American (but not South American) eyes have quite outweighed incidents like Theodore Roosevelt's "taking" of Panama.

Cultural and sentimental considerations have also played a part in the American attitude. Actually, the intellectual and artistic bonds between the English-speaking and the Latin parts of the New World are slight. Despite persistent and well-financed efforts to exchange university students, to arrange lectureships, to distribute books, and to facilitate the travel of editors and politicians, contacts remain somewhat artificial and decidedly thin. Yet something has been accomplished. The United States has produced a large body of students of Latin-American history and institutions, and the books of C. H. Haring, Eugene Bolfort, Frank Tannenbaum, J. M. Callahan, J. Fred Rippy, W. S. Robertson, and others are deservedly esteemed. Two State universities, those of Texas and California, have built up particularly large collections on Hispanic culture in the New World, which are increasingly used. Spanish long ago displaced German as a subject for study in high schools and colleges, and may yet threaten French for first place. A good deal of the best Spanish-American fiction has been translated for northern readers.

Much, too, has been done to create a feeling of hemispheric solidarity. When the United States declared war on Germany in 1917, eight Latin American states followed her example, while five others broke off diplomatic relations with Berlin. Since then the movement for parallel action in matters vitally affecting the New World has gone farther, and was given emphatic and far-reaching formulation by the conferences at Lima in 1938 and at Havana in the summer of 1940.

But although Americans attach this special importance to hemispheric relations, their attempts to woo the southern republics were long singularly untactful and blundering. Indeed, down to 1929 American policy towards Latin America did not even show consistency. Sometimes no policy existed, and, as one Secretary confessed, "We just jumped each hurdle as we came to it". An Administration

like Cleveland's would lay the foundation of a genuine
friendliness, and then an Administration like Harrison's
would wreck the new edifice. The expansionist tendencies
of the United States in the years after 1897, coupled with the
dollar diplomacy of the Taft Administration, created a deep
distrust to the southward. Even Wilson's Administration,
though actuated by the highest motives, made errors which
kept the old suspicions regarding the "colossus of the north"
alive. Americans thought much more about law, order, and
efficiency, about the consolidation of political institutions,
than did their neighbours. For many decades the United
States had adopted the policy of always recognizing *de facto*
governments, without involving themselves in the question
of legitimacy. But Secretary Seward delayed recognition in
order to discourage hasty revolutions; Secretary Evarts
went farther, and made recognition of a new government
conditional to some extent upon the fulfilment of international obligations; and President Wilson went farther
still, declining to recognize a regime (like Huerta's) not
based on moral principles.

After the World War, moreover, those in charge of American policy failed in general to realize that new wine had
been poured into the old bottles. That is, they failed to
comprehend the fervour and strength of the movement for
a social and economic revolution in Mexico, Chile, and other
republics, and to accept the fact that vested interests,
foreign as well as domestic, must necessarily be injured by
the rising tides of social reform and nationalistic sentiment.
Two principles came into almost inevitable collision: the
American demand for the protection of investments which
had been made in good faith, and the native demand for
conservation of national resources against alien exploiters, a
fairer distribution of property, and greater social justice.
The result was that the United States was put into the
position of defending its dollar-interests against long overdue
reforms. Not until Dwight Morrow went to Mexico City as
ambassador in 1927 did a brighter era dawn.

It should be said, however, that some critics of the United
States have made altogether too much of the dollar as a
factor in its Latin-American policy. It is true that economic
considerations have long been potent—as they ought to be.
The natural results have flowed from the fact that the

United States, a rich and expansive nation with an expanding economy, stands next door to weak and sparsely populated countries with opportunities for investment. Particularly in Mexico and Cuba, considerations of propinquity, historic interest, and complementary production have aided in bringing about a huge American investment. Most of it, of course, has been beneficial to both parties. Americans, too, have been fully awake to the fact that if any European Power gained an emphatic ascendency over the economic life of Argentina, Brazil, or Mexico, it might also soon gain a political ascendancy. It would be safer for the United States to obtain the dominant economic position—or at least for America and Britain to share it. Especially about the Panama Canal, investments were deemed to be one mode of safeguarding strategic interests. But, as we have seen in discussing dollar diplomacy, for only a brief period did Washington lend itself to a really predatory type of economic imperialism. At various times it has sharply discouraged predatory interests.

In the years just following the World War, America's principal difficulties with Latin America arose out of her relations with Mexico. That republic had undergone a momentous revolution. After nearly thirty-five years of unbroken power, the dictator Porfirio Diaz had been driven into exile in 1911. Under his "strong-arm" rule, investors had been cordially welcomed. American interests had taken so large a share of the natural resources of the country, particularly in oil-fields and ranch lands, that their holdings were conservatively estimated to be worth £250 millions. The disappearance of Diaz ushered in a series of factional struggles, marked by bitter fighting and many cruelties. Amid the violence the poverty-stricken masses, most of them mere peons or serfs on the lands held by their ancestors, began struggling upward towards a better estate.

With the aspiring masses Wilson sympathized warmly, and although he made errors, his policy genuinely assisted the Mexican people in moving towards a better destiny. But the struggle of the dispossessed had just begun to run its course when Wilson went out of office; and the great majority of propertied Americans persisted in misunderstanding it. They pictured all Latin-American revolts in the same colours, as mere struggles for selfish power on the part

E (N.)

of rival generals and politicos. That is, they did not distinguish between *coup d'états* of the type amusingly satirized by T. S. Stribling in *Fombombo* and true popular uprisings. They did not comprehend that the ragged, hungry peon was just beginning to gain control of land that was his by right; that the oppressed workman in the cities was at last demanding the justice won by his American prototype; and that the paralyzing grip of the Catholic Church on education was being broken. In short, feudalism was rapidly being destroyed in one of its last great strongholds. As this upheaval took place, patriotic Mexican leaders were resolving to check the foreign exploitation of oil and land, and to bring the best resources of the nation under its own control.

This movement was an irresistible tide which no American Government could stop by Mrs. Partington gestures. It could have been halted only by war, which would have meant occupying and administering the country as Japan has taken over Manchuria. The new Article 27 written into the Mexican Constitution to nationalize the subsoil resources of the country was simply one item in the broadfronted revolution. The new agrarian programme for breaking up the great estates into small farms was simply another item. But they pressed so hard on American oil, mining, and ranching interests (including those of W. R. Hearst) that a vociferous demand for intervention arose in certain quarters. It gained support from not a few American Catholics.

By 1926, when President Coolidge and Secretary Kellogg were managing affairs in Washington and Calles was in control in Mexico City, the controversy between the two nations had become extremely irritating. The State Department asserted that the Mexican legislation was "retroactive, confiscatory, and contrary to the principles of international law and equity". The Mexican Government replied that its laws were purely domestic and were an entirely proper expression of its national sovereignty. We need no touch the details of the wrangle, except to note that the principal dispute was over a statute which required American oil-land owners to exchange their titles for fifty-year leases. "Confiscation!" shrieked the oil companies. "A fair equivalent!" responded the Mexicans. Most American interests accepted the new law, but among those which di not were corporations controlled by powerful men: Doheny, Sinclair, Mellon. Finally a complete *impasse* was reached. Kellogg and his ambassador were so uncompromising in their communications that many feared the quarrel would lead to war.

That fear was not abated when Coolidge asked his old Amherst College classmate, Dwight Morrow of J. P. Morgan & Co., to go to Mexico City as ambassador. A Morgan partner seemed of all men the least likely to reach a settlement. "After Morrow", prophesied a Mexican editor, "come the marines." But the event proved happily otherwise. The new envoy was a man of tact, cultivation, and liberal outlook. As Harold Nicolson writes in his biography of Morrow, it was soon clear to the most suspicious Mexican that he had come not to sneer, but "to placate, to appreciate, and to please". He shrewdly induced Colonel Lindbergh, fresh from his dramatic flight to Paris, to make a non-stop flight from Washington to Mexico City. The aviator met such an ovation that one American newspaper proposed that all foreign affairs be assigned to the flying corps. Morrow also brought down the inimitable Will Rogers, whose merry quips eased the tension. Moreover, the ambassador took two steps which at once sharply differentiated him from his predecessor. He made a genuine effort to win the friendship of President Calles, a conscientious and constructive statesman who had been grossly maligned in the United States. And before making any speeches or presenting any notes, he undertook a study of Mexican law and tried to learn the Mexican point of view.

In the end, Morrow—met more than half-way by Calles—completely disposed of the oil controversy. His method showed characteristic sagacity. A number of American corporations had instituted litigation in the Mexican courts to vindicate their rights, and had obtained favourable decisions from the lower tribunals. Morrow knew that if these decisions were upheld in the Supreme Court, under the constitutional provision that no law should be applied retroactively, the basis for a settlement would be laid. He presented this fact to Calles. To his delight, the latter remarked that the kind of decision desired might be expected within two months. Whatever the reflection carried by this statement upon the independence of the highest court of Mexico, it was very reassuring as regards American–Mexican friendship. Calles proved even better than his word. Within a fortnight or so the court handed down a decision holding essential parts of the petroleum legislation unconstitutional, and the Mexican Congress immediately amended the law to fit this decision. The State Department then announced that the voluntary Mexican steps "appear to bring to a practical conclusion discussions which began ten years ago". And if the problem of the American-owned ranches was not solved, it was at least deferred and mitigated.

Altogether, despite the fact that no agreement was reached on the difficult question of Mexico's bonded debt, Morrow's ambassadorship was brilliantly successful. It threw a roseate glow over the whole of American relations with the Latin republics. And when Herbert Hoover displaced Coolidge in the White House, feeling between Mexico and the United States continued to grow in cordiality. This was partly because the new ambassador in Mexico City, J. Reuben Clark, carried forward Morrow's policy of friendly understanding; it was partly because the Hoover Administration adopted an enlightened attitude in all its Latin-American dealings, and squarely abandoned the old interventionist policies.

As a symbol of his desire for a warmer friendship, Hoover immediately after his election made a circuit of all the principal Latin-American ports. At the same time J. R. Clark, then Under-Secretary of State, was writing a long historical exposition of the Monroe Doctrine, which the Administration presently published. It was notable chiefly for its flat repudiation of the "Roosevelt corollary", under which the United States had acted as general policeman of the Caribbean area. Clark accurately declared: "The Doctrine states a case of the United States vs. Europe, and not of the United States vs. Latin America. ... So far as Latin America is concerned, the Doctrine is now, and always has been, not an instrument of violence and oppression, but an unbought, freely bestowed, and wholly effective guarantee of their freedom, independence, and territorial integrity against the imperialistic designs of Europe." This did nothing to recognize the Latin-American desire to make the Doctrine a matter of multinational concern, or to assuage the resentful feeling of the larger republics that they did no want a protector—that, as one man indignantly put it, "We don't need a papa!" But on other counts it was reassuring.

In dealing with the Chaco dispute between Bolivia and Paraguay, a thorny controversy which finally ended in war, the Hoover Administration showed eagerness to collaborate with the principal South American nations, and with the League. On both counts this pleased South America, some of whose republics (notably Argentina) were inclined to value the League as a possible shield against imperialistic designs on the part of the United States. When in 1929 a revolt broke out in Mexico, Washington embargoed shipments of arms to the rebels, while allowing the regular Government to be supplied. The uprising soon failed. The following year the United States pursued the same policy with regard to a Brazilian revolt. But here the rebels gained power; and the Hoover Administration promptly recognized them. In other words, it swung back to the old American principle of recognizing de facto governments without looking into their morals—a reversion which again pleased Latin America.

But above all, the Hoover Administration proved its good intentions and good sense by beginning the withdrawal of American marines and financial supervisors from the Caribbean area. We must say its good sense; for the policing of the five Central American republics and the three island republics of Cuba, Santo Domingo, and Haiti had simply not paid. The theory had been that these eight little nations, like Panama, might be kept orderly and prosperous by a modest display of force. But the order had been precarious at best, while prosperity cannot be conquered by arms. The main results of the interventions had been loss of life, widespread local antagonism, and the creation of a deep suspicion throughout South America.

It must be re-emphasized that the American Government had a difficult rôle to play. Ample evidence exists that before the World War Germany would have been glad to fish in troubled Caribbean waters, and it was good policy not to let them get too troubled. American citizens had a right to protection. The chronic disorders in Haiti had become so appalling just before American troops were sent in that regard for elementary considerations of humanity demanded some action. And in various republics certain elements really wanted intervention. A "legation guard of marines" that was kept in Nicaragua from 1912 to 1925 would have been withdrawn at an earlier date had the Nicaraguan Government not urged from time to time that it should stay on, for its withdrawal would have meant a bloody revolt. When sent away, it soon had to be brought back. But a feeling gained ground in the United States that a less meddlesome attitude towards the little nations was needed; a feeling strengthened by the great depression after 1929, when Americans had no money to invest abroad and were engrossed in their domestic troubles.

Hoover's dislike of intervention was shared by his Secretary of State, Henry L. Stimson, who as agent for Coolidge in Nicaragua had had an opportunity to observe at firsthand how badly the old policy worked there. Indeed, Stimson, by working as mediator between the two warring factions and getting them to agree upon an election under American auspices, had restored a fair degree of peace in the little republic. Only one rebel leader, named Sandino, continued to urge hostilities. The Hoover–Stimson policy of limiting American commitments throughout the Caribbean area rapidly bore fruit. During 1929–31 Sandino continued his cruel guerrilla warfare. But instead of dealing drastically with him, Stimson in the spring of 1931 issued a noteworthy proclamation to American citizens in Nicaragua. He warned them that the United States could not undertake their general protection throughout the country with armed forces. "To do so would lead to difficulties and commitments which this Government does not propose to undertake." Those who did not feel safe were advised to withdraw from the republic, "or at least to coast towns where they can be protected or evacuated in case of necessity".

In accordance with this decision, the American forces (which three years earlier had totalled 5480 men) were gradually extricated, until early in 1933 the American bugles sounded their last call under Nicaraguan palms. The home public accepted their removal with relief. They have not since gone back.

A similar course was followed in the other troublesome little republics. In the spring of 1931 a revolt broke out in Honduras. Following the new Hoover–Stimson policy, the Government announced that its forces would limit themselves to assuring the safety of American lives and property in the coastal towns. Disorders flared up in Guatemala at almost the same time. Again Washington rigidly abstained from any gesture in the direction of intervention. In Haiti, where our marines still lingered, serious rioting took place in the last days of 1929. Hoover contented himself with asking Congress to supply funds to send an investigating commission to the island. His instructions to Cameron Forbes, who headed the body, were: "The primary question which is to be investigated is when and how we are to withdraw from Haiti. The second question is what we shall do in the meantime."

The commission reported that most of the Haitians wished to see the American occupation terminated—and terminated it was. The American high commissioner was replaced by a regular minister, steps were taken for the progressive Haitianization of the government services, and in 1932 a treaty to end the regime was signed. Because of some restrictive features, the Haitian congress refused to ratify it. Though it was therefore left to Roosevelt to complete the evacuation, the credit for ending an unfortunate episode goes chiefly to the Hoover Administration. The last marines left the island in 1934. Armed forces had long since departed from the Dominican Republic under the treaty of 1924. The Caribbean was now fairly free of Uncle Sam's policemen in khaki—and everyone concerned hoped that it would remain so.

It will be seen that the Hoover Administration had laid a foundation upon which Franklin D. Roosevelt, entering the White House in 1933, could readily build; and he did so with very remarkable success. In his inaugural address he declared: "In the field of world policy, I would dedicate this nation to the policy of the good neighbour." It was a happy phrase, and Secretary Hull was ready to help give it meaning by happy acts. Fair words alone would never have won the goodwill of the southern republics, who had heard too many of them. But the aims and spirit of the New Deal, as revealed in the first year of the Administration, caught the liking of the more advanced Latin American nations— Mexico, Chile, Uruguay. It soon became plain that Roosevelt and Hull meant to interpret the Monroe Doctrine in a way that would not offend Latin America; that they meant to warn all interlopers, and particularly the totalitarian states, away from the New World; and that they intended to avoid intervention or other meddling. Before many years passed their policy aimed at the establishment of a common front by all the American nations in facing a troubled world.

The first evidence that the good-neighbour policy would return golden dividends appeared at the Montevideo Conference in December 1933. This Pan-American gathering took place at a gloomy moment. The great depression had settled down upon the whole world, the Economic Conference had just failed in London, and the Disarmament Conference seemed on the point of collapsing at Geneva. But the Montevideo meeting was a striking success. All the American republics but one were represented. Ten, including the United States, sent their foreign ministers. As soon as the delegates had an opportunity to measure Hull's mind and character, they showed a remarkable willingness to trust him. Hull astonished and pleased them by his readiness to discuss a Mexican proposal aimed at "super-bankers" and their "worm-eaten system of credit". He dryly remarked that "the international bankers, as a rule, are not and have not been supporters of the Roosevelt Administration". He manifested a similar spirit when the vexed question of intervention was brought forward. An elaborate convention for defining the rights and duties of states was submitted. It contained the following clauses:

> Article 8. No State has the right to intervene in the internal or external affairs of another.
>
> Article 11. The contracting states definitely establish as the rule of their conduct the precise obligation not to recognize territorial acquisitions or special advantages which have been obtained by force, whether this consists in the employment of arms, in threatening diplomatic representations, or in any other effective coercive measure. The territory of a state is inviolable and may not be the object of military occupation nor of other measures of force imposed . . . for any motive whatever even temporarily.

Hull cordially subscribed to this, asking only that the terms of Article 8 be defined. He declared that he felt safe in saying that "no government need fear any intervention on the part of the United States under the Roosevelt Administration". The Montevideo Conference adopted no fewer than 114 recommendations for the promotion of inter-American amity. A resolution for the removal of trade barriers, including high tariffs, was particularly noteworthy. Altogether, Hull was justified in saying that the meeting "thoroughly demonstrated the success of international conference as a method of settling important questions and advancing the general welfare". Roosevelt firmly supported Hull's stand in disclaiming any wish to keep intervention alive. Two days after the conference adjourned, he declared that "the definite policy of the United States from now on is one opposed to armed intervention", and added that if orderly government broke down in any country, that "becomes the joint concern of the whole continent in which we are all neighbours".

Montevideo was a great landmark in New World history. And other steps soon followed. In his message to Congress at the beginning of 1936 Roosevelt declared that the good-neighbour policy was "a fact, active, present, pertinent, and effective". He immediately thereafter proposed to the other republics a special Conference on the Maintenance of Peace, which met in Buenos Aires in the last weeks of 1936. To this conference he journeyed in person, addressing the initial session. Hull was again head of the American delegation. Though Argentina showed a certain jealousy of American leadership, once more the gathering proved harmonious and successful. Its most important result was a Convention for the Maintenance, Preservation, and Re-establishment of Peace, which provided for general inter-American consultation if any threat of war touched the New World; whether war with an Old-World nation, or war between two American countries. The document contained at least a germ of the "continentalization" of the Monroe Doctrine, converting it from a national into a multinational doctrine. A treaty on the prevention of controversies set up a number of mixed commissions between American republics to devise means of avoiding future conflicts. Moreover, a new protocol raised still higher the barrier against intervention. It asserted that the American nations acknowledged as inadmissible "the intervention of any one of them directly or indirectly and for whatever reason in the internal or external affairs of any other of the parties". The American Senate promptly ratified the peace convention or consultative pact.

Meanwhile, the United States had furnished some practical illustrations of its good neighbourliness. Cuba was cursed with a brutal dictator named Machado. His removal became absolutely imperative. But Roosevelt handled the situation with masterly tact. Two months after his inauguration he sent Sumner Welles to the island. This experienced diplomatist offered to mediate between the dictator and his opponents, and using as his very effective lever the negotiation of a commercial treaty which was expected to help rescue Cuba from her economic difficulties, he carried through a plan of adjustment which included Machado's withdrawal. A series of presidents and dictators have followed Machado, the most important being the former army-sergeant Batista, now in power. The United States managed to avoid conflict with any of them, although Washington made its disapproval of one, Grau San Martin, emphatically clear. At every important step in his necessarily complicated dealings with Cuba, Roosevelt has consulted the representatives of Argentina, Brazil, Chile, and Mexico, explaining his acts and aims.

Moreover, in 1934 the United States made the somewhat overdue decision to abolish the Platt Amendment and the practical protectorate which it had established over Cuba; an act long demanded by liberal elements in both countries. This was done by a treaty of "general relations". At the same time the President signed an executive agreement, authorized by Congress, which put into effect the system of reciprocal preferential tariffs which Welles had helped to work out. In negotiating these tariffs a genuine effort had been made to serve the interests of the small republic. Cuba was now genuinely independent, mistress for good or ill of her own destinies.

In Mexico the old disputes between the oil companies and the Government had meanwhile, as a result of drastic labour legislation, entered upon a new phase. The companies were soon insisting that the wage rates imposed by Mexican statutes were ruinous, but the Mexican Supreme Court upheld the labour authorities in demanding payment of them. Finally, in March 1938, President Cardenas expropriated outright all the foreign oil holdings, valued at about $400 million. This was perfectly legal, and was not improper if a fair compensation was paid; but grave doubts were felt about payment. The British Government took steps which led to a breach of diplomatic relations. The American Government, though hard pressed by clamorous American investors, and irritated by the fact that much of the oil was bartered to Germany, did nothing more than make vigorous representations. Roosevelt and Hull treated the Mexican Government with consistent courtesy, made the most of an agreement by Mexico in the autumn of 1938 to pay for expropriated agricultural lands, and by continuing the silver-purchasing policy through 1940, provided Mexico with a welcome amount of revenue. Relations have remained cordial, and early in 1941 Vice-President-elect Wallace attended the inauguration of the new Mexican President.

Thus was the good-neighbour policy firmly established, and in the nick of time. For by 1936 the villains in the drama had appeared—and villains darker than the authors of the Monroe Doctrine had ever imagined. The German Nazis had begun a strenuous campaign to convert Latin America to their economic ideology. In this they were abetted by Italy and Japan, which, like Germany, had sent large bodies of settlers into South America and had built up banking and commercial agencies there. Germany and Italy presented a natural market for the raw materials of South America. They rapidly expanded plans under which they bought and paid for them not in money but in barter credits, good for manufactured goods from the Axis lands. British and, to a lesser degree, American exports suffered. Germany also, with increasing boldness, demanded the acceptance of Nazi dogmas; Latin-American export firms were asked to dismiss their Jewish employees, and to hand over important business posts to Nazi agents. American traders vociferously complained that Axis competitors were using the most unfair methods to gain a grip on trade.

But what most alarmed the United States was the political threat which lay behind the economic encroachments. Radio programmes of Nazi and Fascist origin carried violent attacks on democratic ideas; lecturers, journalists, and authors were marshalled to assail the United States; films were adroitly used; the German and Italian minorities in various lands were sedulously organized by cultural and athletic societies that had a political and even military character. Propagandists and political agents swarmed over Latin America, exploiting every element of discontent. The Roosevelt Administration felt a growing alarm. It asked Congress in 1938 for a special appropriation to support a radio programme, which was refused. It saw that the various Federal departments and such agencies as the Maritime Commission laboured tirelessly to strengthen the ties of Pan-American unity. With the Nazi–Fascist threat uppermost in his mind, Secretary Hull took a carefully-selected delegation to the Eighth Pan-American Conference at Lima in the closing days of 1938.

Zones of warmth—so the British Commonwealth of Nations and the Latin-American family seemed to worried Americans as they looked out upon an increasingly chilly and jangling world. It was a world in which zones of potential hostility had existed in the Far East and Central Europe ever since the World War; and as the great depression crept over the globe, these zones became actively and threateningly hostile.

WORKING MEN'S COLLEGE LIBRARY

CHAPTER IV

ISOLATIONISM

WITH its immense economic and naval strength, and with its increasing confidence in the friendly support of the British Empire and the nations of Latin America, the United States might have been expected in the decade 1929–39 to play a bold and statesmanlike part in international affairs. That it refused to do so is to be attributed primarily to the strength of the isolationist elements in the nation. An analysis of isolationism, and of its rôle in the middle thirties in attempting to legislate a cast-iron neutrality, is essential to any understanding of American foreign policy.

The bases of American nationalism or isolationism are varied. Some are geographic: the thousands of miles of salt water that separate the republic from Europe and Asia. Some are economic: the immense mineral and agricultural resources of the continent, rendering it all but self-sufficient. Some are political: for the founders of the nation cherished a suspicion of Old World Powers, and the course of European events has deepened this suspicion, so that leaders from Jefferson to Borah have preached the avoidance of Old World entanglements. Some may be called social: millions of Europeans fled to America to escape the restrictions, injustices, and poverty of their lot, and their descendants naturally desire, in many instances, to hold aloof from the old continent. Nothing could be more fatuous than to regard isolationism as intellectually contemptible. On the contrary, its doctrines attract many scholarly and thoughtful Americans.

The economic arguments presented by the nationalist school, for example, cover a number of interesting points. They assert (1) that free trade belongs to the past, and fitted only one country, Britain, in one special period (1845–1914), during which she held a fairly clear lead over the rest of the world in industry. The Manchester doctrine of free trade was based on the idea that each nation and region ought to produce those commodities for which it was best adapted;

but the advance of science and technology has now placed many nations on roughly the same footing, enabling each to produce nearly all that it needs for home consumption. International exchanges have thus become far less important than previously. They will continue to decline in importance. The rise of synthetic industries, for example, has made Germany independent of rubber, and America of silk, while tin may soon be replaced by lacquers on steel cans.

The nationalists declare (2) that the pressure of unemployment makes the old economic internationalism impossible. Whenever men lose their jobs, they will force the Government to raise trade barriers to restore employment; *e.g.*, the Smoot–Hawley Act and the Ottawa Agreements. They maintain (3) that currency difficulties also make the doctrines of Adam Smith unworkable. Uneven exchanges and depreciation create trade barriers, and a long period of international monetary stability will be essential before men can even talk of free commerce. They argue also (4) that free trade is out of date not merely on economic grounds, but on political and military grounds. The moment a country sees war or the danger of war looming ahead, it will fly to a nationalist instead of an internationalist economy. It has to do so to assure itself of survival if beleaguered. They assert (5) that nations which attempt to keep the markets of their neighbours open by force are likely to provoke armed resistance. And finally, they insist (6) that the profits of free international trade are often illusory. The United States in 1920–29, for example, sold large quantities of valuable goods for bad paper.

On the social side, also, the arguments of the American isolationists run a good deal deeper than many of their critics suppose. They point out that the United States represents a medley of national stocks, as yet very imperfectly fused, and that as yet the republic has not gained a distinct personality—not found its soul—as older lands like England and France have done. Time and quiet are needed for this process. The country cannot achieve a distinct culture and character unless it is kept insulated from distracting outside influences. For this reason it has sharply limited European immigration. For this reason many of its writers, artists, and thinkers have inveighed against a sterile imitation of the Old

World, an intellectual colonialism. And for the same reason it should take care not to be drawn into political entanglements with European nations, into alliances and conflicts that will retard the achievement of its true destiny. The republic can best benefit the world by becoming more truly *American*.

In all this there is some force, if more of sophistry and tendentious thinking; and it is easy to understand why, after the defeat of the League, such ideas gained ground. They were supported by selfishness, timidity, and inertia. The stay-at-home policy was easier, cheaper, and at first blush safer than the bold policy of aiding in world-organization. Isolationist tendencies were supported also by the old smug America-is-better-than-Europe sentiment. And partisan considerations also played a large rôle. The principal cause of the defeat of the League unquestionably lay in factors of party politics. Many Republican leaders cherished a fanatical hatred of the Wilson Democrats; many powerful business captains feared that peace would bring a resumption of Wilson's reforms. These two groups were natural allies. They made the most of popular discontent with the war burdens, the general ignorance of the Versailles Treaty, the Irish and German rancours, the widespread dislike of Wilson, and the tradition of American isolation. Aided by the President's own intransigency, they committed the nation to abstention from the League.

Beginning in 1929, with the onset of the great depression, the prospects for world co-operation rapidly deteriorated. Caught in the howling economic tempest, most lands turned to an accentuated nationalism. The international currency and exchange system almost collapsed; world trade shrank to a trickle; desperate tariff wars were opened; and governments shamelessly defaulted on their debts. In the widening chaos, many Americans thought isolation the only safe road. They even debated a policy of autarchy. Normally about one-tenth of American production had been for foreign markets, and that fraction had meant for many industries the difference between prosperity and loss. But it seemed so narrow a margin that it might conceivably be given up. In their bewilderment many citizens were eager to forget the outside world, and attend exclusively to domestic affairs.

Their feeling was strengthened by a systematic campaign

of isolationist propaganda which, already some years old, showed three main elements. One part of it was devoted to strengthening the disillusionment and discontent which had followed the war. It preached that the country had been tricked into entering a capitalistic and imperialistic struggle. Another part described, with great exaggeration, the injustices bound up in the treaties of Versailles, St. Germain, and Trianon, and in their execution. A third part dealt critically with the question of German war-guilt. Some writers pushed revisionism so far as not merely to make France and Russia partners in the guilt, but to suggest that next to Britain, Germany was the most nearly innocent of all the powers.

The Republican party was predominantly isolationist. It is true that President Hoover, who had supported the League in 1920, and Secretary Stimson, were internationalists by innate conviction. So were a few other prominent Republicans. Elihu Root in a public address of 1928 sharply condemned the course of his party with regard to the League. Sympathy had been denied to it and to the World Court, he declared, during years in which they had "been rendering the best service in the cause of peace known to the history of civilization; incomparably the best". Nicholas Murray Butler at the same time remarked that the isolationism of the previous Administrations had "made this nation of ours a dangerous derelict across the path of every ship that sails laden with the precious cargo of international friendship and accord". Hoover and Stimson in the years 1929–33 permitted an increasing participation in the non-political labours of the League. By the beginning of the latter year the American Government had taken part in literally scores of League conferences, and had appointed hundreds of delegates to them. In dealing with the narcotics problem and the traffic in women, Americans had given the League a strong progressive impulse.

But in general, the ichor instilled into the veins of the party by Borah and Lodge had done its insidious work. Few of the leaders were willing to go farther on the international road than the cautious station represented by the Kellogg–Briand pact. This weak and largely futile instrument had an interesting American background. For years a movement for "outlawing" war had been promoted by

Salmon O. Levinson, a Chicago lawyer who was encouraged by Senators Borah and Knox among others.
Early in 1923 he introduced into the Senate a resolution
proposing that war should be made a public crime, that
international law should be codified, and that a powerful
international court should be created. The idea might not
have borne fruit but for a scholar of imagination, James T.
Shotwell. He helped to indoctrinate Aristide Briand, the
receptive French foreign minister, with the idea of outlawing
war. Thereupon Shotwell and Nicholas Murray Butler
forced the plan upon public attention; Senators Borah
and Knox converted the reluctant State Department; and
Secretary Kellogg, becoming enthusiastic, pressed a multilateral treaty upon all the nations.

But no implement whatever was provided to give the
renunciation of war valid effect. It was merely a pledge,
which any nation athirst for revenge or spoliation could
break like gossamer. Those who hailed it with delight over-
looked the fact that it did not commit the nation to the
risks and sacrifices indispensable for the object sought.
During the debate, various Senators had proposed that at
least some machinery for consultation should be set up.
But Borah and others resisted all these efforts, asserting that
the aroused public opinion of mankind would be weapon
enough. That Borah was sincerely concerned nobody can
deny. "When shall we escape from war?" he demanded
once during these years. "When shall we loosen the grip of
the monster? That is the most stupendous problem in the
world today. Beside this question all other questions are
subsidiary and elementary. Without a solution, and a
favourable solution, of this riddle, human progress becomes
a misfortune, the inventions of the human mind a curse, and
civilization, so called, an alluring trap into which men and
women are ensnared to a death of unspeakable torture."
Borah had thought in 1920 that the League went too far.
He thought in 1928 that the Kellogg–Briand Pact went far
enough. He lived to see that on both points he had been
tragically in error.

The Democratic Party remained so strongly tinctured
with Wilsonian ideas that when it returned to power in
1933, the way seemed open for a new advance towards
internationalism. Both Roosevelt and Hull belonged

emphatically to the internationalist school. Though the former had said in the pre-convention campaign that the United States should not enter the League, he was known to believe strongly in the principle of collective security. He and Hull carried forward the energetic American co-operation with the non-political activities of the League, already so well launched. In the economic sphere, Hull won a signal victory for liberalism in his reciprocal trade agreement law. The new Administration also indicated its willingness to place an embargo upon the trade of nations which violated the Kellogg Pact, for its spokesman, Norman Davis, declared:

> We are willing to consult the other states in case of a threat to peace, with a view to averting conflict. Further than that, in the event that the States, in conference, determine that a state has been guilty of a breach of the peace in violation of its international obligations and take measures against the violator, then, if we concur in the judgment rendered as to the responsible and guilty party, we will refrain from any action tending to defeat such collective effort which these states may thus make to restore peace.

But Roosevelt and Hull found progress along the main road of internationalism at first impossible. The bad world-situation, the recent tradition of inertia, the suspicions deeply implanted in the public mind were insurmountable. As the rise of Hitler and the truculence of Japan presaged new wars, the obsessing idea of the American people was to stay out.

This attitude expressed itself by 1934 in a powerful demand for laws to safeguard American neutrality if any new conflict began. The impulse behind this demand was born primarily from the scowling world-scene and the sabre-rattling of the dictators. But other elements contributed. Early in the year Senator Nye of North Dakota introduced a resolution calling for an investigation of the munitions industry in America. He was applauded by many voices. A spate of books and articles was being poured out at the time upon the arms business throughout the world; and a long paper which *Fortune* published in March, 1934, describing in graphic detail the manufacturers, their government connections, their intrigues in Europe and America, and their profits, was especially influential. In April, 1934, the Senate set up the desired investigating committee with Nye as chairman. Its work lasted for nearly three years.

The findings of this committee covered broader ground and made a deeper impression than had been anticipated. Its most important inquiries concerned two matters: the structure and methods of the munitions industry, and the economic background of the American drift to war 1914–17. All the hearings were widely publicized.

The committee had no difficulty in showing that excessive profits had been made during the World War by bankers, arms-makers, and supply services generally. It reported that the activity of various shipbuilders, wherever examined, "was close to being disgraceful". It proved that many industrialists had been guilty of questionable practices in obtaining contracts, filling them, and terminating them when the conflict ended. It demonstrated that tax-dodging had been practised by such means as artificial changes in contract-dates. Army and navy officials were convicted of gross carelessness in scrutinizing cost-sheets. Coming down to more recent times, the committee presented facts which tended to disclose something like an international combination of armament dealers, active in obstructing efforts towards peace. It proved that American munitions firms had eagerly pushed the sale of arms to foreign lands, including potential enemies of the United States; and that the War and Navy Departments had facilitated such sales, because they kept the industry alive and vigorous.

Particularly sinister, in the eyes of many observers, were the disclosures regarding America's entry into the World War. The activities of J. P. Morgan & Co., which had handled nearly all the allied purchases in the United States, were explored. It was shown that when the United States joined in hostilities, the Allies owed debts of $2,700,000,000 in the country; that American industry was largely geared to Allied needs; and that Allied defeat would have struck a heavy blow at American prosperity. Had the nation gone into the conflict of its free volition to save democracy?—or had it been pushed into the furnace by greedy munition-makers and bankers? The Nye Committee had a positive answer. Its final report declared that selfish financial and industrial interests had built up so heavy a stake in the Allied cause that "it prevented the maintenance of a truly neutral course between the Allies and the Central Powers".

All this was grossly exaggerated. The United States went into the World War because, first, for numerous good reasons American sentiment was from the beginning strongly enlisted on the Allied side; and second, and above all, because the Government took a course in demanding respect for its time-honoured neutral rights which, when Germany began her submarine warfare, led inexorably to a conflict. But an effective book had already presented the Nye thesis in a way that captured a wide public. Walter Millis in *The Road to War* (1935) argued that the machinations of profiteers, the pro-Ally bias of Wilson and his advisers, and the naïveté of Colonel House, had been largely responsible for the plunge into battle.[1] In vain did Newton D. Baker publish a volume pointing out how determinedly neutral Wilson had been, and showing that German infractions of neutral rights were the main cause. When Robert Lansing's *Memoirs* appeared with a frank confession that, as Secretary of State, he had been determined from the outset to see Germany defeated, a host of Americans took the Nye–Millis view. They did not realize that Lansing had never been important enough to determine or strongly influence foreign policy.

Confidence in the wisdom of all Presidents in handling foreign affairs was shaken by these attacks on Wilson. Congress was isolationist; Roosevelt and Hull were internationalist. Would it not be well to curb even Roosevelt? A more radical nationalism, with stress on economic implications, was soon being expounded in various books: Charles A. Beard's *Open Doors at Home*; Clark Foreman's *The New Internationalism*, and Jerome Frank's *Save America First*. Thus it was that the demand for legislation to safeguard American neutrality became irresistible.

The final fate of the World Court in the Senate showed which way the wind was blowing. The old project for American adherence, with a plenitude of safeguards attached, had been brought forward once more. The best leaders in both parties endorsed it, and Roosevelt gave it warm though not militant support. But a swarm of isola-

[1] Millis in a pamphlet, *The Faith of an American*, Oxford University Press, 1941, takes a very different line with the present war.

tionists, Anglophobes, and hundred per-centers descended upon Washington. The Hearst press thundered, and Father Coughlin crooned hate over the radio. When a vote was taken in January, 1935, the Court bill was once more defeated—not to be revived. Roosevelt, alert to all the trends of public feeling, perceived that he must bow to neutrality legislation. Indeed, a measure of some sort, if only to meet certain plain defects in the existing laws, was imperative. Charles Warren, who had been assistant Attorney-General under Wilson, published a widely-read article in *Foreign Affairs* for April, 1934, in which he pointed out some of the respects in which the United States had left herself peculiarly exposed, and suggested a programme of legislation to lessen the risk of embroilment. His first four points were:

1. Take over all high-power radio stations; forbid foreign ships to use radio in American waters.
2. Forbid the sale of arms and ammunition to belligerents.
3. Prohibit the shipment of arms and ammunition on American vessels, and forbid American citizens to travel on ships laden with munitions.
4. Forbid armed merchantmen to enter American ports, and forbid American citizens to travel aboard them.

It at once became plain that Congress and President differed on the essential character to be given the neutrality legislation. There were clear signs that war was imminent in Ethiopia, and might spread to Europe. Congress wished to erect insuperable barriers against the export of arms and ammunition, laying down rigid rules applicable to *all* belligerents. Roosevelt, seeing that conflicts were likely to arise between aggressor states and peace-loving victim states, wished to be in a position to carry out the policy enunciated by Norman Davis; to help in "collective effort" against "the responsible and guilty party". That is, he wished the law to vest a wide discretion in the President, enabling him to deter or cripple aggressors and to aid their victims. Early in 1935 he had the McReynolds bill introduced in Congress—a bill which kept the principal reins in his own hands. It empowered him to place an embargo on "shipments of arms, ammunition, and implements of war" whenever a conflict began abroad, and authorized him to designate the nation or nations to which this embargo would apply. He might also forbid American ships to enter a war zone, might prohibit loans to belligerents, and might warn Americans that they travelled on the vessels of belligerent nations at their own risk.

This discretionary power would have given the President a powerful new weapon, the war embargo, to employ in his diplomacy. He might brandish it at will against Germany, Italy, or Japan if they threatened to take a lawless course, and might use it to support the League. But Congress would have none of his plan.

No fewer than fifteen neutrality bills were introduced in the two houses; and after much weary disputation in the hot summer of 1935, Congress hammered out a rough measure of the most rigid character. It prohibited the export of arms, ammunition, or implements of war to any belligerent nation, or to any country which might trans-ship to a belligerent. It made it unlawful for an American vessel to carry arms for or to any belligerent. It authorized the President to warn American citizens that they travelled on the ships of belligerent powers at their own risk. The President was allowed no authority to discriminate between righteous and wicked, aggressor and victims. He was given some latitude in choosing the moment to make the law effective; in defining the term "arms, ammunition, and implements of war"; and in extending the embargo to states which might become involved in the conflict as it progressed. But apart from this his hands were tied.

Roosevelt would have fought the measure had he not been assured that he would meet defeat—and had he not been anxious to keep Congress in good humour over his domestic programme. He signed it with a protesting statement that it might well "drag us into war instead of keeping us out". Events showed that he would have acted wisely had he vetoed it.

The new law did not operate badly in the first conflict to which it applied, the Italo-Ethiopian War. Of course Roosevelt and Hull strongly sympathized with Ethiopia. The President quickly proclaimed an embargo effective upon both nations. But Ethiopia could obtain arms from the League powers, while Italy was really handicapped by her inability to buy munitions in the United States. When Americans were warned off ships of the two countries, no Ethiopian liners suffered!—and Italian liners did. The President had no power to prevent Americans from selling Italy valuable collateral war materials—cotton, copper, scrap-iron, rubber, and oil. But he did indicate to the League powers that he would support their sanctions against Italy; and in pursuance of this design he warned citizens that such trade was contrary to national policy, and that the Government was closely watching all shipments. This amounted to a moral embargo. The United States made it clear that it would have co-operated with the League in stopping oil shipments to Italy (which took little American oil anyway); and the primary reason for the breakdown of opposition to Mussolini lay in Anglo-French vacillation.

Yet even so, the Neutrality Act had an unfavourable effect upon the situation. Evidence exists that when the British Ministry was weighing the chances of war with Italy, its tendency towards caution was accentuated by its knowledge that this law was on the statute books. British and French leaders knew well that if they had to fight Mussolini, the United States would withhold arms and ammunition from them. Mussolini knew it too.

As Italy completed her shameless conquest of Ethiopia, the international situation continued to deteriorate. Indeed, after that triumph of brute power the League as a political force was practically dead. Americans naturally showed a deepening desire to keep out of the stormy affairs of Europe. Haile Selassie had hardly fled when trouble broke out at a new point, in Spain. The revolt which Franco and other conservatives launched against the Madrid Government in July, 1936, swiftly gathered strength. The United States had seldom concerned itself with civil wars abroad, and was largely indifferent to this conflict. A Gallup poll soon showed that while 22 per cent. of the people favoured Madrid and 12 per cent. the rebels, 66 per cent. either had no opinion or were neutral. As a matter of fact, the Spanish war shortly became more than a civil conflict. Russia on one side, Germany and Italy on the other, took a free hand in the fighting.

The Neutrality Act had said nothing about civil wars, or wars partly civil, partly foreign. This was a dismaying oversight. The State Department at first undertook to remedy it by using moral suasion on arms exporters not to sell to either party. When its measures proved ineffective, Congress rushed through a joint resolution (approved January 8, 1937) which forbade the direct or indirect export of arms to Spain. This would have been fair enough if Britain and France had succeeded in getting other governments to observe the non-intervention agreement which they signed. Doubtless when Roosevelt approved the resolution he thought that they would succeed, thus lessening the peril of a general war. But Germany and Italy broke their pledge, sending in both munitions and men. The result was that the American embargo worked heavily to the disadvantage of the Madrid Government, which might otherwise have obtained much-needed supplies in the United States. Even Senator Nye grew unhappy when he saw this, and introduced a bill to raise the embargo for the Spanish loyalists alone. Ex-Secretary Stimson supported the proposal. But the State Department failed to do so, and Congress was quite unwilling to act. The embargo did not safeguard American neutrality, for that was never really threatened; it did not shorten the conflict; it merely played into the hands of Germany and Italy in Spain, and contributed something to the overthrow of democratic government in that land.

While the Spanish conflict was dragging to its end, and while Japan was preparing for a new assault upon China, interest in neutrality legislation remained acute in America. This was necessarily so, for the law of 1935 expired on May 1, 1937. Congress took the subject up anew with all its old prejudices unabated. Faith in collective security now seemed almost dead in America. It was hopeless for the President to try to obtain a discretionary law, permitting him to discriminate between good and bad belligerents. Roosevelt doubted whether he could even obtain discretion to fix the date when the embargo should be applied. Congress was again determined upon a rigid statute, and determined also to take action covering the accessory commodities vital to modern warfare—cotton, copper, scrap-iron, and so on.

The result was the act reluctantly signed by the President on May 31, 1937. Setting up an elaborate new scheme, it was designed to protect American neutrality more com-

pletely than ever. It retained the embargo on arms, munitions, and implements of war to *all* belligerents, good or evil.
It retained a provision enacted by joint resolution in the
spring of 1936, making it unlawful to buy or sell belligerent
securities after the date of a neutrality proclamation. It
made travel by Americans on belligerent ships unlawful.
It permitted the President to extend the embargo to any
civil war which threatened the neutrality of the United
States. But its most important new feature was the "cash-
and-carry" provision, prescribing a "come and get it"
neutrality.

This provision, which Bernard M. Baruch is credited with
inventing, applied to the accessory munitions like cotton,
scrap-iron, and oil. Americans were unwilling to give up
their sale, yet they were as important in fighting as high-
explosive. After a war began such materials (the President
was to make a list) could not be shipped to or for a belligerent
in an American vessel. The President could also require
that they be paid for before they left the United States. All
loss, if they were sunk or captured, would thus fall on the
foreign purchaser. It was an ingenious plan, but, being
wholly novel, it was limited to two years.

This neutrality Act of 1937 registered the high-watermark
of isolationist sentiment and power in the United States. In
the spring of 1937 nationalist feeling seemed completely
ascendant, international ideas either dormant or dead.
This was in spite of the clear wishes of Roosevelt and Hull,
who wanted a discriminatory embargo so that they could
threaten international malefactors. It was in spite of such
Republican leaders as Henry L. Stimson; in spite of such
publicists as Hamilton Fish Armstrong and Allen W. Dulles,
who presently published in *Can We Stay Neutral?* a strong
indictment of the legislation. It was in spite of many others
who shared Hull's view that the United States had sub-
stituted "a wretched little bob-tailed, sawed-off domestic
statute for the established rules of international law". It was
in spite of the demonstration that in the Ethiopian conflict
the legislation had exercised a dubious effect, and in the
Spanish conflict had been worse than dubious. But the
isolationists rejoiced. Many of them believed that a sovereign
specific for keeping the United States out of foreign entanglements had been found.

The purpose of the legislation, triumphantly wrote one isolationist, was "the greatest possible insulation of the United States from foreign wars". If the Administration conformed to the act, he added, it might be concluded "that such insulation could be achieved". Peace would result. How fatuous was this hope the next few years were to show. They were also to show that, once the error of the legislation was exposed, the retreat of the American people from it could be swift and emphatic.

CHAPTER V

NATIONALIST *vs*. INTERNATIONALIST

THE internationalist school of thought has long been powerful in the United States, and even in 1937 was much stronger than it seemed. It might better be called the world-cooperationist school, and the fact should be emphasized that it covers a wide gamut of opinion. In this broad sense, it has numerous and influential leaders. In the Democratic Party they include most of the principal figures, from Roosevelt, Hull, and Henry Wallace downward; in the Republican Party such important men as Henry L. Stimson, Frank Knox, Nicholas Murray Butler, and Charles E. Hughes. Numerous journals, headed by the New York *Times* and *Herald-Tribune*, the Philadelphia *Record*, and the Chicago *Daily News*, and prominent publicists, such as Walter Lippmann, William Allen White, and Chester Rowell, argue for the cause. World cooperation is upheld with pen and voice by a large body of university professors: James T. Shotwell, Manley O. Hudson, Quincy Wright, and many more. The diplomatic service is full of its adherents, and Winant, Bullitt, the late William E. Dodd, and Norman H. Davis have given it devoted labour.

Politically, the internationalists believe that peace cannot be achieved by a static policy: that it must represent dynamic and unresting labour on a world-wide scale for the achievement of freedom, justice, and security. They emphasize the need for organizing peace; that is, for a system of collective security backed by a unifying ideal. They hold, in general, that the best way to keep the United States out of war is to help prevent any war from beginning; for in any conflict of major proportions the United States will as inevitably be involved as it was in the Napoleonic Wars and the World War. They accept and develop the principle laid down in Article XI of the League Covenant, that war anywhere is a matter of concern to all nations everywhere. While they would not suppress nationalities, they point to the need for some organization which will assure their cooperation for the common good, while restraining lawless nations and policing the world. Most internationalists have been friends of the League of Nations, although many believe that it needs revision and rehabilitation, and some would not have America join without careful safeguards.

In the economic field, this school vigorously rebuts the arguments offered by the isolationists. It asserts that since modern life has made the needs of every progressive people highly varied and complex, free international trade has become more a necessity than ever. Present-day industry requires such materials as tungsten, platinum, tantalum, manganese, vanadium, chromium, aluminium, asbestos, mica, helium, and molybdenum. In many instances the supplies are narrowly localized. As Charles W. Cole points out, most of the world's helium comes from Texas, seven-tenths of its tungsten from South America, and half of the chromite from Southern Rhodesia. Nations in the temperate zone find it hard to dispense with tropical products like rubber, coffee, chocolate, spices, lacquers, tropical fruits, and tropical drugs. Even the United States cannot do without a wide variety of overseas products. It uses more tin, rubber, coffee, bananas, and silk than any other land, and imports nearly all its supplies. What of England? What of Germany? What of Japan? They need a wide variety of raw materials brought from overseas. Moreover, as industrial nations they must sell their products abroad or face loss and unemployment. The United States must also send its surpluses of cotton, tobacco, wheat, and meats into foreign trade, or it will face a terrifying problem of internal adjustment.

The internationalists argue that a world organized to permit freer trade will be a more prosperous world. Nations that exchange goods which they do not want for goods which they do will have a higher standard of living. The world will also be more peaceful. The great depression of 1929–39, assert the internationalists, was attributable in large part to trade barriers. The United States had led the way in erecting high tariffs; other nations had set up import quotas, exchange controls, and barter agreements. The result was to check the currents which made for prosperity, to arouse discontent, and to create a basis for imperialist wars. Germany, starved of what she needed, began

VI. INTERNATIONALISTS

1. SECRETARY FRANK KNOX : NAVY (*Black Star*)
2. SECRETARY HENRY L. STIMSON : WAR (*Black Star*)
SECRETARY OF STATE CORDELL HULL WITH LORD HALIFAX (*Wide World Photos.*)

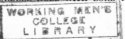
WORKING MEN'S
COLLEGE
LIBRARY

demanding *Lebensraum*, Japan prepared to bring Eastern Asia under her domination. In short, economic warfare results in armed warfare. Hitler was quite right when he said that Germany must export or die. Free trade and international peace lend each other mutual support. By the liberation of trade the ordinary internationalist means:—

1. Tariff, quota, and exchange barriers should be lowered (not necessarily abolished).

2. All nations must have access on equal terms to all kinds of raw materials.

3. All nations must have access to markets for their goods.

In the social field, the internationalists emphasize the value of a free interplay of culture. They do not deny that the United States should try to form a clear-cut national character; they do not wish to overtax the melting-pot. But they want the United States to take a friendly and generous attitude towards other peoples, their ideas and ways. They point out the immense value of the non-political contacts at Geneva; the interdependence of nations in education, art, and intellectual affairs generally; and the folly of believing that true Americanism is incompatible with an assimilation of the latest advances abroad. Several American organizations—the Institute of International Education; its daughter-body, the American University Union in Europe; the Division of Intercourse and Education of the Carnegie Endowment—have done invaluable work in promoting cultural relations with the Old World. They have done much to show that internationalism enriches, while isolation impoverishes, the mind of America.

In their effect on international relations, the economic policies of the Roosevelt Administration were decidedly confused. This was chiefly because the New Deal was an *ad hoc* programme, itself full of inconsistencies and contradictions. Part of it was designed to give the United States a greater national self-sufficiency. Part of it looked towards the re-establishment of freer trade and a better international division of labour. Secretary Hull by no means saw eye to eye with all other Cabinet members, or at all times with the President himself.

Nothing illustrated this fact better than the abortive World Economic Conference held in London in 1933. Hull unquestionably hoped for large results from this gathering. It was to consider: (1) monetary and credit policy; (2) prices; (3) renewal of the flow of capital; (4) lowering of trade restrictions; (5) tariff policy; and (6) organization of production. In advance of the gathering, the British, French, and Italian Governments sent distinguished agents to Washington to try to reach some agreement upon a programme. All eyes were then fixed upon the London sessions, which Hull attended as head of an able group. But it proved a fiasco. Just before it opened Roosevelt had taken the United States off the gold standard in order to raise prices at home and meet foreign trade competition abroad. He refused to allow the United States to join the other leading nations in stabilizing their currencies—that is, to peg the dollar. The sessions broke up with no real accomplishment beyond a minor agreement on silver-purchasing.

Yet as the unremitting advocate of tariff reduction the world over, the undiscouraged opponent of mercantilist policies wherever they appeared, Hull continued to do admirable service for economic internationalism. He defeated or wore down every foe in the Administration. He imposed his will upon Congress. American prosperity, he said, depended upon his policy: "full, stable, and durable business recovery can only be effected by the restoration of international trade and finance to an extent mutually profitable." Once Congress had given him authority to write reciprocal trade agreements with other nations, he used it pertinaciously—and by 1940, when his powers were renewed for the third time, he had put all scoffers to rout.

The first trade agreements were easily reached with Latin-American countries on whose exports the United States had placed few duties: Brazil, Colombia, Guatemala, Haiti, Honduras, Nicaragua, Salvador. While the United States retained or enlarged the free lists on their goods, they took American motor-cars, machinery, and other commodities under reduced duties. Then Cuba joined the roster. The one-fifth reduction in all duties which she had received under the Platt Amendment was confirmed to her, while she lowered her tariffs on American textiles, machinery, motor-cars, and some agricultural products. When an agreement was undertaken with Canada, vigorous opposition appeared in the United States. Representatives of farming, lumbering, and mining interests protested that Dominion competition would be ruinous. Nevertheless, the agreement went through. Meanwhile, powerful manufacturers rose in arms as negotiations were undertaken with the highly industrialized nations of Europe. But Hull quelled or ignored their revolt, signing conventions with France, Belgium, Holland, Sweden, Switzerland, Czechoslovakia, and, above all, Great Britain.

Much debate has raged around the question of the value of these trade agreements to the American economy. Up to 1939, the State Department had reduced the duties on some 411 imported commodities. It had pushed about half of the rates lower than those in the Fordney–McCumber Act of 1922, and about one-sixth of them lower than those in the Underwood Act of 1913. This was encouraging progress in tariff reduction—even though the tariff covers about 3200 commodities in all. Such statistical evidence as was available indicated that the United States had increased its export trade by the Hull programme. Moreover, the agreements had created a psychology favourable to further tariff slashes, for public sentiment unmistakably supported them. They strengthened the forces in the United States favourable to an expanding capitalist economy.

And whatever their internal effect in America, they were of unquestioned value to international goodwill. As we have pointed out, they contained clauses by which the United States extended gratuitously to all nations (unless guilty of discrimination) every advantage offered by any reciprocal trade agreement. Future concessions were also to be broadly bestowed. If Switzerland, for example, made a reciprocal treaty with Britain by which duties were lowered on British cars, that reduction would automatically extend to American cars. The Hull programme thus made for a general loosening and lowering of trade impediments throughout the world. It wrote one of the brightest pages in the dark history of the time.

The political course of the Roosevelt Administration in international affairs was more consistent than its economic course. It is true that Roosevelt signed the successive Neutrality Acts, which a more rigidly internationalist President

—Wilson, for example—would have vetoed. It is true that he also signed the Johnson Act of 1934, providing that no person under American jurisdiction might make a loan to any government that had defaulted on its debt to the United States. This sealed up private sources of credit in the United States to Britain, France, and other lands. Roosevelt might also be reproached for refusing to make a really determined fight for the World Court. On the other hand, he saw that the United States continued to take a full part in the many humanitarian, cultural, economic, and technical conferences held under League auspices. He gladly cooperated in making the United States a partner in the International Labour Office at Geneva. If he accepted the neutrality legislation, it was with repeated and emphatic protests. And beginning in 1937, the Administration began to take a much stiffer attitude towards the aggressor nations.

It first showed its inclination to follow a stronger line of action in dealing with Japan. Its policy in the Far East was a fairly direct continuation of that followed by Hoover and Stimson. The story of Japanese–American relations in the thirties offers an exceptionally significant illustration of the difficulties of international cooperation.

Since 1899 the United States had been committed to the protection of the Philippines and the maintenance of the Open Door in China. It had gone into the Far East under a curious complex of motives. As other countries owned colonies, many people had thought that the United States should have a few—notably the Philippines. The Spanish War, McKinley wrote, had "brought us new duties and responsibilities which we must discharge as becomes a great nation". The idea that Germany or Russia might get the islands if America did not take them irked the republic. Commercial considerations were also prominent. Just before the war the Bureau of Foreign Commerce had spoken of the bright prospects for "an American invasion of the markets of the world", with "immense gains to our manufacturers", and had declared that China presented one of the most promising fields. An American banker wrote a magazine article declaring that half the people of the earth lived in countries easily reached from the Philippines. The chance of converting the Igorrote thrilled numerous churchmen. But one fact is to be made emphatically clear: no Americans

G (N.)

thought of the Philippines as a stepping-stone to further territorial gains.

Nearly all the bright hopes pinned to the islands and to the Open Door proved illusory. The anticipated trade with China failed to develop, so that American exports to that country in 1939 were much below those to Venezuela. It was with Japan that a rich trade grew up. The Philippines did not strengthen the naval position of the United States, but weakened it. It was obvious that they could not be defended long against Japan. Nevertheless, having made its policy, the United States had to carry it through. The Open Door was part of a fundamental tradition of the republic. The little brown brother in the Philippines needed thorough tutelage, and although Washington repeatedly proclaimed its intention of releasing the islands in good time, it was not until 1934 that it fixed a date ten years ahead—and that date was subject to revision.

Some unselfish motives also played a part in American policy. The desire to maintain China's territorial integrity, to improve Chinese education and health, and to foster Chinese democracy, reflected a pervasive American idealism. The churches, the Rockefeller boards, and other agencies spent tens of millions in the Orient. American experts, with youths educated in American universities, encouraged republican institutions. This admixture of altruistic impulses with material aims has always lent a special fervour to the American attitude towards China. Dollar gains have been few. But Americans cannot forget the spirit behind Hay's insistence that China should not be partitioned, the schools, colleges, missions and hospitals with which they have dotted the land, or their hopes for a democratic republic there. They like the Chinese people and their culture far more than they like the Japanese.

As the guardian of the Open Door, the United States was bound to become the opponent of what Japan called her rightful aspirations, and what Americans termed a policy of selfish aggression. During the first twenty years of the century tension between Japan and America rapidly increased. The Japanese were displeased by the outcome of the Portsmouth Conference which Theodore Roosevelt called to end the Russo-Japanese War. Commerical friction developed in Manchuria. Japan, deeply sensitive to any hint of racial inferiority, also resented the landholding laws of California and the immigration policies of the United States. For a time the Root-Takahira agreement of 1908 seemed to erase nearly all differences. But during and just after the World War feeling grew more acute than ever. The United States resented the famous twenty-one demands of Tokyo on China, and the occupation of Shantung. Japan resented Wilson's refusal (along with Great Britain) to include a declaration of racial equality in the League Covenant. The American and Japanese forces sent to Siberia, ostensibly to rescue a Czechoslovak contingent, got on so badly that when the last American troops sailed away from Vladivostok, the Japanese band struck up "Hard Times Come Again No More". A quarrel developed over the former German island of Yap. And American writers began issuing sensational books on the new yellow menace—books like Walter Pitkin's *Must We Fight Japan?*

The Washington Conference in 1921 temporarily did something to ease the situation. It ended the danger of a naval race. It did away with the irritating Anglo-Japanese alliance, substituting for it a compact by which Britain, Japan, the United States, and France agreed to respect each other's rights in the Pacific, and to refer disputes to a joint conference. It drafted the Nine-Power Treaty pledging these four nations and five others to uphold the "sovereignty, the independence, and the territorial and administrative integrity of China", and to maintain the Open Door. The signatories did not agree to *defend* China's political and commercial independence by force; they merely agreed not to attack it. Indeed, the American Senate by an explicit reservation disavowed any obligation to use force to protect the status quo in the Orient. As a reward for accepting the 5–5–3 ratio in capital ships with Great Britain and the United States, Japan received a promise that America would not strengthen the fortifications on any of her Pacific Islands except Hawaii; that is, on the Philippines, Samoa, Guam, or the Aleutians. A spirit of genuine amity marked the close of the Washington gathering.

Yet many difficulties and dangers remained. It soon became clear that the gains made in limiting armaments were but transient. While a ten-year holiday in the building of capital ships had been decreed, no restrictions were placed on smaller craft, and competition shifted to them. At the end of ten years the agreement was only partially extended, and in 1934 was denounced by Japan. As for the protection of China and the *status quo* in the Orient, that also was precarious; for the Japanese fleet was left without any equal antagonist in Far Eastern waters, and if Tokyo chose to break her word, could do much as it pleased. The promise not to fortify the Far Eastern islands irked Admiral Sims, who made the disgusted remark: "Anybody can spit on the Philippines, and you can't stop them." A much stronger guarantee of Chinese integrity and the Open Door than the Nine-Power Treaty was really needed; a guarantee that only the League of Nations, and a League made strong by American membership, could have offered.

We may of course distinguish two great periods of crisis in the Far East: one the crisis of 1931–32, ending in the erection of Manchukuo, and the other the crisis which began in 1937 with a new Japanese invasion of China. The former found President Hoover and Secretary Stimson in charge of American policy. Following an alleged explosion on the Japanese-controlled railroad near Mukden on the night of September 18, 1931, Japanese troops quickly overran all South Manchuria. They acted with a precision which pointed to a well-matured plan. What was the United States to do? The Nine-Power Treaty was clearly being violated, the Open Door was being menaced. Should America take a stern attitude, ally herself with the League, and threaten Japan with economic coercion by embargoes if not with open war?

Secretary Stimson was hampered by various factors. One was the fast-deepening economic depression, which half paralyzed the energies of the United States. Another was the attitude taken by Hoover. As a man of Quaker stock, a former mining-engineer who had worked in the Far East and a former Secretary of Commerce who had kept in close touch with business interests, Hoover had clear-cut ideas of his own. A few weeks after the Japanese onslaught he treated the Cabinet to a memorandum on the situation. He asserted that the "whole transaction is immoral". He added, however, that he did not despair of China, for "the Chinese people possess transcendent cultural resistance"—they would expel or absorb the invaders. Thereupon he se himself to point out the natural limits upon American action. It was true that Japan was using outrageous violence and was smashing a solemn treaty. The United States had a moral obligation to support the Nine-Power compact, and to co-operate with the rest of the world, including the League, in this endeavour. But should America consider going to war if the efforts of the League failed? Hoover's answer was an emphatic No. "These acts [by Japan] do not imperil the freedom of the American people, the economic or moral future of the people. I do not propose ever to sacrifice American life for anything short of this. . . . We will not go along on war or on any of the sanctions either economic or military, for these are the roads to war." On that emphatic statement Hoover stood fast.

Several other factors also restricted Stimson's range of action. One was his firm conviction that if the more liberal Japanese leaders, such as Baron Shidehara, were not bullied and humiliated by the Western Powers, they would be able to keep the aggressive army and navy groups under control, and find a moderate solution for the Chinese problem. Stimson, who had also lived in the Far East, retained a considerable faith in the older Japan. Another difficulty lay in his lack of any practical experience with the League machinery or methods. Still another restriction, as events soon showed, was the unwillingness of the British Foreign Minister, Sir John Simon, who was close to the "City", to co-operate completely with Stimson. The result of all these circumstances was that when the State Department did move, it failed to achieve unity with the League, to gain wholehearted British support, or to impress Japan with its earnestness. In the end Geneva, London, and Washington were all left disconcerted and baffled.

The League's first impulse was to send an investigative commission to the seat of trouble. But Stimson discouraged this undertaking, declaring that the United States could not approve such an investigation or admit that the Kellogg Pact had been violated. Unquestionably he did this because he feared that a sharper course would weaken the moderate element in the Japanese Ministry. The London *Times* commended him; League circles condemned him. Clarence K. Streit wrote to the New York *Times* from Geneva that "No one on the inside is likely ever to forget the deep gloom and bitter disillusionment that overwhelmed League officials then, while the Japanese grew arrogant." He concluded that the favourable moment for bringing Japan up short "had gone forever". Other American supporters of the League have characterized Stimson's action as a fatal blunder. But he acted according to his best judgment. He immediately made a statement expressing "wholehearted" sympathy with the general League effort; and it is certain that after this first difference, he was ready to cooperate loyally with Geneva by taking parallel (not joint) action.

In this cooperative spirit, Stimson authorized the American consul in Geneva to attend the Council meetings there as observer and auditor. A month later Ambassador Charles G. Dawes was sent to observe the Council deliberations when they reopened in Paris. He smoked and debated at the Ritz Hotel while the Council members smoked and debated at the Quai d'Orsay. Various emissaries dashed back and forth between the two seats of authority. Some writers have treated Dawes's failure to attend the League deliberations (as he was authorized to do) as most unfortunate. In effect, they declare, he set up a rival agency of his own—he upholding the Kellogg–Briand Pact while the Council strove to uphold the Covenant. Dawes himself controverts this view, and in his published diary takes much credit to himself. Both the Chinese and Japanese representatives, he writes, after receiving messages from their governments which if presented would have created an impasse, "would first bring the matter to my attention". Dawes and Simon would also exchange calls. "This made it possible for me on several occasions to exercise an influence in preventing impasses which might have occurred. . . ."

But apparently Dawes achieved his results by bringing heavy pressure on the Chinese. John T. Whitaker witnessed the exchanges, and gives us a condemnatory verdict in his book *And Fear Came*. He writes that it was vital for the United States to impress the Japanese with the belief that America was determined to see China through, and that Dawes "gave exactly the opposite impression". In the end, no settlement was reached at the Paris deliberations. Japan became more unyielding; and when the Council appointed the Lytton Commission to investigate the dispute, the Minseito Cabinet fell.

As Tokyo grew more stubborn, and as Japanese armies crushed the last Chinese resistance in Manchuria, Hoover and Stimson moved to a stronger expression of disapproval. On January 7, 1932, Stimson enunciated in identical notes to China and Japan the doctrine which has since borne his name. This document, which Hoover helped to draft and which had a number of American precedents, asserted that the United States "does not intend to recognize any situation, treaty, or covenant which may be brought about by any means contrary to the covenants and obligations of the Pact of Paris"—*i.e.*, by force. Copies were sent to the British and French ambassadors, with a hint that the United States hoped for parallel action by London and Paris. Naturally, France waited for a British lead. It failed to come. Instead, the British Foreign Office rebuffed Stimson by issuing a press communique which expressed confidence in Japanese intentions, and asserted that the British Government would take no action along the American lines. That same day the London *Times* printed an editorial pooh-poohing the idea that Japan would set up a regime in Manchuria hostile to foreign business interests, and declaring that it was not the immediate business of the Foreign Office to defend the administrative integrity of China, for that integrity did not exist. In short, the *Times* went far towards justifying Tokyo's course.

And to the end the story remained one of cross-purposes and confusion. When in January, 1932, the Japanese began their butchery in Shanghai, British opinion swung to an abrupt *volte-face*—for Shanghai was the centre of large British interests. American opinion was deeply stirred. The main American fleet was now in Hawaiian waters. Many observers expected a close Anglo-American cooperation. Many hoped for a clearer identification of the United States with the League's efforts. Apparently Stimson shared the belief that Britain and America might act together, and was sustained in that confidence by certain talks with Simon over the transatlantic telephone. He has frankly avowed in his book *The Far Eastern Crisis* that he wished to encourage the League to impose economic sanctions upon Japan, and hoped that Congress would take similar action. But an embargo upon shipments to Japan, he thought, would be more readily adopted by Congress "if it were recommended following the invocation of the Nine-Power Treaty than if it had been recommended solely by the League of Nations".

Stimson therefore invited the British Government to join the United States in invoking the Nine-Power Treaty to "focus the moral support of the world upon the situation which had taken place in Shanghai". He pressed the invitation urgently by telephone. But Simon flatly refused. Much debate has since taken place upon the question whether Simon, after first encouraging Stimson, deliberately let him down. It is clear that Stimson thinks he did. But time may show that Simon possessed good reason for his course. He perhaps preferred to act with the League, which had not yet recommended or even considered sanctions, rather than under the Nine-Power Treaty. And he was perhaps not prepared to take so far-reaching a step unless he had fuller assurances that Hoover and Congress would support Stimson in carrying through the imposition of sanctions. No such assurances could have been given, for Hoover had made it clear that he was unwilling to approve of economic sanctions, believing them a certain prelude to war, while Congress was in an isolationist mood. American Press opinion, as careful analyses showed, was then against any Japanese boycott.

Thus brought to a halt, Stimson found a vent for his emotions in a letter to Borah, in which he intimated that Japan's treaty-violations had now set the United States free to increase its navy and strengthen its Pacific bases. The League Assembly by formal resolution adopted the Stimson doctrine of non-recognition. Japan withdrew from Shanghai, but refused to evacuate Manchuria, and in September, 1932, converted the province into the puppet state of Manchukuo. Late in 1932 the Lytton Commission made its report, and when it was adopted by the League a few months later, Japan indignantly withdrew from that body. The United States, Great Britain, and the League had all met defeat in dealing with the aggressive leaders in Tokyo, and their discomfiture was to have the gravest consequences. If the western powers, acting through a really strong League in which the United States was a loyal member, could have taken prompt and united action, they could easily have brought Japan to a halt. Their failure to act together advertised the weakness of the Covenant and showed that the Kellogg Pact was but an empty formula. Hitler and Mussolini took careful note of the lessons taught by Japan. Within a few years Hull could truthfully declare that the attempt to disintegrate modern civilization had its beginnings in Manchuria in 1931-32.

The new crisis in the Far East opened in July, 1937, with an outbreak of fighting between Japanese and Chinese troops near Peiping. It found the main outlines of the international situation radically altered—and from the American point of view, altered for the worse. The feebleness of the League had been completely demonstrated by the tragic events in Ethiopia. It was left discredited and powerless. Great Britain's hands were tied fast by the menacing situation in Europe. She could hardly spare a glance to the Far East, and certainly could not send any considerable part of her armed forces there. France was in a similar predicament. The United States now faced Japan substantially alone, and the Japanese Government knew it.

While Hoover and Stimson had not always seen eye to eye in Oriental affairs, Roosevelt and Stimson were in perfect accord. Both men were deeply aroused as fighting spread to Shanghai, with a horrifying loss of life among the innocent people of that great city ; both were anxious to use every instrument for hampering Japan and assisting China. But it was clear that the Japanese invasion of one province after another could be stopped only by force, and the United States was not prepared to use force. The Spanish crisis was drawing near its unhappy climax, and deeply alarming Americans by its disclosure that Europe, and indeed the world, was sitting on a heap of dynamite. The summer of 1937 witnessed a severe economic relapse in the United States. The naval race with Japan had been recommenced in 1936, and Tokyo was building heavily in those categories which would be most useful for defence. While the outcome in a Japanese–American war could be predicted with certainty, the conflict would cost heavily in lives and money—and America's interest in the Orient would not justify the expenditure.

The anomalous character of the Neutrality Act was demonstrated anew by the crisis. The law stipulated that "whenever the President shall find that there exists a state of war", he should proclaim the fact. But he did not find

that war existed in China, though the deaths there soon ran
into hundreds of thousands. Moreover, his refusal to issue
a proclamation had the approval of the great majority of
the American people. Since neither Japan nor China
formally declared war, the President had a technical justification for his course. But it was merely technical; the
authors of the law seem to have intended that it should apply
to declared and undeclared hostilities alike. Indeed, during
the hearings on one of the early bills Assistant-Secretary of
State Moore had firmly asserted that it was the President's
duty to issue a proclamation whenever a war "actually
occurred". Now, however, Senator Pittman, who had taken
a great part in writing the 1937 law, explained that no such
duty existed. Japan, he said, was disseminating a disease of
aggression which might spread to the rest of the globe, and
should therefore be quarantined "as every civilized com-
munity quarantines against contagious disease". The
Neutrality Act was never intended to offer such a quarantine. Its object was "solely to eliminate certain causes which
might lead us into a foreign war".

Though the neutrality legislation had clearly not been
applicable to the Spanish war, special action had been taken
to apply it there. Though it was clearly applicable to the
Chino-Japanese war, care was taken not to apply it there.
Obviously, the legislation was more flexible than it seemed.
If it served a purpose desired by the American people and
Government, it could be invoked; if not, it could be
neglected.

The fact was that to impose an arms embargo in 1937
would have done little injury to Japan, while striking a
heavy blow at China. Japan is a highly industrialized
country; she can manufacture her own arms, warships, and
airplanes if she is only given the necessary raw materials—
and the neutrality law did not cut off raw materials. But
China had few factories. She badly needed arms, ammunition, tanks, and airplanes from foreign countries. Not only
that, but she needed the money to purchase them, and the
oil to keep the major engines of war going. Had Roosevelt
proclaimed the neutrality of the United States, he would in
effect have been taking sides against China—that is, com-
mitting an act which went far to assure the triumph of the
aggressor. Law or no law, such a course would have seemed
intolerable to most Americans.

Yet the President and Hull were at various points still in advance of American opinion—an opinion quite as strongly on the isolationist side as British opinion still seemed on the appeasement side. They would have taken positive steps to hamper Japan. But the public, while strongly sympathetic with the heroic Chinese, was anxious to avoid any involvement. Under pressure of opinion, Roosevelt warned Americans that if they stayed in China they did so at their own risk. A Gallup poll in September, 1937, showed that 54 per cent. of the voters favoured withdrawing all marines and other armed forces from China. Trade counted for little as compared with American lives. And the trend of American feeling was strongly displayed when Roosevelt on October 5, 1937, made his "quarantine" speech in Chicago.

This address had a background of League action. An American representative was now sitting with the League's Far Eastern Advisory Committee; and on October 5 the committee adopted a resolution declaring that Japan had violated the Nine-Power Treaty and the Kellogg Pact, and recommending a conference of the powers. Hull immediately announced that the conclusions of the American Government were in general accord with those of the League. It could hardly have been a mere coincidence that Roosevelt chose October 5th for his Chicago speech. Taking a strong stand against international lawlessness, he declared that countries which contributed to gangsterism and disorder should be quarantined. "The peace, the freedom, and the security of 90 per cent. of the population of the world is being jeopardized by the remaining 10 per cent., who are threatening a breakdown of all law and order. Surely the 90 per cent. who want to live in peace under law and in accordance with moral standards that have received almost universal acceptance through the centuries, can and must find some way to make their will prevail. . . . There must be positive endeavours to preserve peace."

Two days later ex-Secretary Stimson came out vigorously for an economic embargo upon Japan. The President's ringing speech was hailed by believers in collective security as a pledge of active co-operation with other nations in stopping Japan—and in discouraging Germany and Italy. But American opinion refused to support Roosevelt. On the contrary, newspaper comment made it clear that until America's vital interests were attacked, the nation would

not approve of armed action, or of any course likely to lead
to armed action. Not even the sinking of the gunboat *Panay*
by Japanese aircraft (December, 1937) aroused the American
people to demand punitive steps. They grumbled, but they
showed no excitement. The next month a fresh Gallup poll
showed that the vote favouring withdrawal of armed forces
from China had grown from 54 to 70 per cent. Because
neither the American people, nor any other people, were
willing to fight to stop Japan in China, the conference of
nineteen powers at Brussels ended in total failure.

Yet as time passed the Roosevelt Administration did go
to bold lengths in its pressure upon Japan. Not merely did
the State Department in various documents, like the note
to Japan on December 31, 1938, emphatically refuse to
countenance the "new order" that Japan was trying to set
up, and assert its reservation of "all rights of the United
States"—that is, of the Open Door. Washington also used
some new weapons. In June, 1938, Hull revealed that he
had unofficially declared a "moral embargo" upon the shipment of airplanes to all countries which engaged in the
aerial bombardment of civilians; and the Government took
steps to make this embargo good as respected Japan. In
December the Reconstruction Finance Corporation announced that the Export–Import Bank had given the
Chinese Government's purchasing agency in the United
States credits to the amount of $25,000,000. A few days
later the Secretary of the Treasury let it be known that the
United States would continue to extend China credit
against gold which it accumulated in America by the sale of
silver. When somebody asked if this contravened the spirit
of the Neutrality Act, he said No. "Who's at war? We are
simply extending credit to a friendly nation."

In short, the United States was not wholly helpless. As
Roosevelt, speaking of aggressor-nations in his message to
Congress in January, 1939, significantly said: "There are
many methods short of war, but stronger and more effective
than mere words, of bringing home to aggressor governments the aggregate sentiment of our people." That same
month the report of the Hepburn Board urged the immediate construction of forty-one bases, chiefly in the Pacific,
fifteen to be built with all possible speed. Several bills were
introduced during the spring to provide for a general

embargo of Japan; and in midsummer the American Government denounced its commercial treaty with Tokyo, so that after the expiration of a year it would be able to apply strong economic pressure. But the United States had not been able to prevent the savage subjugation of a great part of China, or the presentation of a grim Japanese threat to Oceania.

This Japanese story constitutes an unhappy chapter in American foreign relations. The moral to be drawn from it seems fairly simple. The United States had an important stake, commercial, political, and sentimental, in the preservation of Chinese integrity and the Open Door. But it was unwilling to fight a costly war for the maintenance of its Far Eastern interests. Under these circumstances, its one hope of preserving them against a powerful and aggressive Japan lay in joining the League, with its general guarantee of the territorial and commercial rights of members, and its economic weapons for protecting them; or at the very least, in cordial co-operation with the League. Unfortunately, for reasons mainly political, the United States had cast the League aside and long refused to have anything to do with it. When a Nine-Power treaty was improvised to take the place of the League guarantees, it lacked any weapons and proved useless. Before the Republican regime of 1921-33 ended, Secretary Stimson had shown the good sense to try to retrace the steps taken and to meet Japanese aggression by bringing the efforts of America into harmony with those of Geneva. But it was too late; Japan was but briefly stayed. Partly because of American abstention from the League in its formative years, partly because of the selfishness and blundering of Great Britain and other member-powers, the forces which might have guaranteed world order had become divided and impotent.

Of course a different view is taken by isolationists, who hold that failure would have been just as inevitable and galling had the United States entered the League; that jealousies and power-politics would have ruined that body under any circumstances, and left America just as helpless in the Far East as before. Some writers hold that American objectives there have been entirely wrong since the time of John Hay, and that it is no concern to the United States whether Japan expands in Asia or not. But these are not the opinions of Secretary Hull. Nor are they the views of Mr. Stimson, whose book *The Far Eastern Crisis* was written in part to teach that American relations with the League must be regularized. In this volume he shows how many advantages League members possessed in approaching Chino-Japanese problems, and under what disadvantages isolated America laboured. "In short," he declares, "they lived in a world purporting to be governed by law and its methods. We still lived in what was little better than a world of anarchy, governed by force or the threat of force." Significant words from a former Republican leader who had become one of the best-trusted members of Roosevelt's Cabinet!

It was Japan which first proved to thinking Americans that isolationism, whether from the international or the strictly national point of view, had serious flaws. Meanwhile, Europe was preparing an even more impressive lesson on the inadequacy of the isolationist policy.

WORKING MEN'S COLLEGE LIBRARY

CHAPTER VI

DEMOCRACY AT BAY

As late as the end of 1937 American policy in Europe might almost be summed up in two phrases: "Neutrality at all costs," and "No commitments!" Mussolini had sponged the kingdom of Ethiopia from the map. Hitler in March, 1936, had suddenly re-occupied and garrisoned the Rhineland, and had denounced the Treaty of Locarno. Both the dictators had intervened in Spain while Great Britain, France, and the United States had refused to allow the Madrid Government to do what was its perfect right under international law—that is, to buy and import arms. As the storm-clouds thus mounted in Europe, the dominant idea of the American people and Congress was to keep out of the almost certain tempest. It was an understandable ambition, and quite as excusable as the campaign for appeasing Germany which was then still gaining vigour in Britain. But within two years the American attitude was to undergo a momentous revolution.

Even from the standpoint of the isolationists, the Neutrality Act of 1937 was far from satisfactory. It contained flaws which showed how impossible it is to control the administration of foreign policy by rigid statute. To begin with, it was not truly neutral. It allowed nations which possessed gold and credits, as Britain and France did but the Axis powers did not, to make purchases in America up to the limit of these resources. The British and French gold reserves were intact, and their nationals owned a great part of the foreign holdings in American properties, securities, and bank-accounts, estimated at $8,000,000,000. Hence they could produce at least a minor war boom in the United States. The law also gave a distinct advantage to the nations which held control of the seas—again Britain and France. They could transport goods under the cash-and-carry clause, while in a war against them Axis vessels could not. The statute allowed American vessels, manned by American crews, to voyage to nations adjacent to belligerent powers; to go to Spanish and Portuguese ports, for example, when Germany was at war with France. If such vessels were sunk, serious consequences might follow.

It was clear, too, that the terminology of the law was loose. The phrase "existence of a state of war" was not precise. It enabled the Government to refuse to act in an undeclared war, such as Japan was waging against China. The phrase "implements of war" was also far from self-defining, and the President might or might not construe it to cover airplane engines, bomb-packing crates, and tele-scopic mounts.

But the principal defect of the law, as farsighted inter-nationalists like Roosevelt and Hull perceived, lay in its flat assumption that if a great conflict broke out between the democracies and totalitarian powers in Europe, the United States ought to stand aside, and could do so. Of course, if the democracies won a quick victory, neutrality would be easy. If the war went into a prolonged deadlock, the two antagonists so closely matched that victory was uncertain, then it would become much harder. America's sentimental attachment to France, her many ties of blood, culture, governmental tradition, and material interest with the British Commonwealth, the loyalty of Americans to the democratic ideal, would evoke a demand that the republic throw her sword into the scales. And what if the totali-tarian powers showed themselves easily the stronger—if they threatened to crush the two great democracies of Europe? What if, allied with Japan, they seemed about to grasp the domination of Europe, Asia, and Africa? What if they threatened to place America in an isolated, precarious, and dependent position? Then the demand for American intervention would become irresistible.

In 1937 few men thought of these dire possibilities. The French army, entrenched behind the Maginot Line, was believed the strongest in the world. The might of the British Empire was well understood. Few observers realized how rapidly and efficiently Germany was arming herself But statesmen trying to legislate a cast-iron neutrality system should have canvassed every possibility of the situation. They should have taken a more realistic view o the fierce strain which would be placed upon American feeling by a deadly grapple between democracy and auto cracy. The fact was that they possessed the wrong kind o

VII. "FREEDOM FIRST"

1. AMBASSADOR WINANT WITH MR. CHURCHILL AND LORD DERBY (*Fox Photos.*)
2. LORD LOTHIAN IN WASHINGTON (*Pictorial Press*)
3. MR. HARRY L. HOPKINS GREETED BY MR. ANTHONY EDEN (*Fox Photos.*)

realism. It was a "realism" which assumed that a war between Germany and Italy on one side, Britain and France on the other, would be simply a new war of selfish power-politics. They did not realize that it might soon seem to most Americans a war between darkness and light, in which it would be treason to the American spirit to stand callously aloof.

For a brief period in 1937–38 isolationism remained in unthreatened ascendancy. Roosevelt and Hull still made utterances in which they tried to awaken Americans to a fuller understanding of the world drift. Hull, for example, penned a letter to Vice-President Garner in which he significantly remarked that the United States had a concern in countries like China which went beyond mere dollars. "There is a broader and much more fundamental interest—which is that orderly processes in international relations be maintained." But the nation was distrustful of every attempted lead. Representative Ludlow brought forward in the House a resolution calling for a popular referendum prior to any declaration of war. Numerous publicists showed how gravely this would fetter the Government and how seriously it would tend to divide the nation in the face of imminent peril: how much it would please Hitler. It commanded so much unthinking support that the President and Secretary of State had to assail it publicly when reported out of committee. It was then remanded, but only by the close vote of 209 to 188. A Gallup poll showed that 70 per cent. of the population apparently stood behind the resolution, and that nearly as large a percentage was opposed to American participation in any form of collective action. According to the Institute of Public Opinion, most Americans desired:

1. A larger army and navy.
2. No entanglements with foreign nations or the League.
3. Action to keep Americans out of belligerent nations.
4. A popular referendum on any war.

Yet slowly at first and then swiftly, the pendulum swung from isolationism to internationalism. Within two years events proved to the hilt that, as Roosevelt and Hull alway believed, isolationism was utterly untenable. These events converted a majority of the American people to the view expressed by Attorney-General Jackson at Havana in March, 1941 : "No longer can it be argued that the civilized world must behave with rigid impartiality toward both an aggressor in violation of the treaty and the victims of un-provoked attack. . . . A system of international law which can impose no penalty on a lawbreaker and also forbids other states to aid the victim would be self-defeating".

When the dictators in Europe took up their rapid march from one conquest to another, American sentiment began really to awaken. The annexation of Austria to the Reich in March, 1938, was accepted with only sporadic expressions of disgust and alarm. The Administration did not apply to it the Hoover–Stimson doctrine of non-recognition of forcible annexations. For one reason, the British and French Governments had readily acquiesced in it; for another, most Americans did not regard the union of Austria with Germany as in itself improper. But it increased the apprehension caused by Japanese aggression in the Far East. One result was to lend vigour to the demand for a far stronger American navy—a navy powerful enough, in fact, to raise a strong shield in both oceans.

Doubtless Roosevelt was thinking both of the European dictators and of Japan when he sent a message to Congress in January, 1938, asking for new naval forces of unprecedented size. He may also have been thinking of the new depression of 1937–38, which a programme of naval construction would alleviate. But he did not say so; he asked for the ships "simple and solely because of the piling up of additional land and sea armaments in other countries, in such manner as to involve a threat to world peace and security". The Administration at first estimated the cost at £220,000,000, and later raised the figure to £288,000,000. It also announced its desire to augment the man-power of the navy by twenty per cent. Congress quickly fell into line. The resulting Naval Act, signed May 17, 1938, authorized an increase in capital ships up to an effective tonnage of 660,000; in aircraft carriers up to an effective tonnage of 175,000; and in cruisers up to an effective tonnage of 412,000. Critics grumbled, but time proved that Roosevelt had been farsighted.

All that summer Europe was filled with rumours of Hitler's intention to deliver a lightning attack on Czechoslovakia. The agitation in the Sudetenland was fanned to fiery heat. In September came the crisis—and the Administration had public sentiment behind it as it took a long new step towards vigorous participation in world affairs.

American interest was whipped to high excitement by a blaring chorus of radio commentators and a clamour of newspaper headlines. The masses in the United States, as in other lands, were desperately eager to see war postponed. No steps were taken by the Government until Hitler, after the Godesburg conference, rejected Chamberlain's proposals for a continuance of negotiations. A conflict seemed imminent. Roosevelt thought it imperative that he throw his moral weight into the wavering balance between peace and war. On Sunday, September 27, 1938, he and his State Department advisers prepared a last-minute appeal. The final touches were placed upon it in the White House study at midnight. It was an urgent plea to Hitler and Benes, in the name of 130 million Americans, to continue their efforts to find a peaceful solution. Naturally, copies were sent to the British, French, and Italian Governments. From Prague, Paris, and London came cordial replies, but Hitler's response was merely a denunciation of Versailles and the Czech people. On September 27th war still seemed imminent. But Roosevelt was ready to make a further effort. That evening he and his associates finished a new message to Hitler, appealing for a conference at "some neutral spot in Europe" to discuss terms of settlement. At the same time, he sent a personal message to Mussolini— to whom Chamberlain was also making an earnest plea. Whether his direct appeal to the Fuehrer had any effect is not known, for no reply was vouchsafed. All that is certain is that Hitler gave way, and that as Chamberlain was speaking to Parliament on the 28th a messenger hurried in with the invitation to Munich.

But if the American people rejoiced over the calling of the Munich Conference, they did not rejoice over its result. The settlement made the very name of that city a term of reproach and bitterness. Disillusionment overspread the nation. The feeling against the Nazis hardened as suspicion of Hitler's aims grew more intense. Roosevelt told his advisers that he "had all his fingers crossed" on appeasement.

The growing antagonism of Washington towards Nazi Germany was dramatically advertised by several occurrences late in 1938. In November an embittered Jew murdered an attaché of the German embassy in Paris. Officially inspired pogroms ensued throughout Germany. Horror and disgust were universally voiced by the American press. Roosevelt determined to take a strong line. Overruling a State Department group which wished merely to send a sharp protest, he recalled Ambassador Hugh Wilson from Berlin "to report". The State Department let it be known that he had been sent for as a rebuke to Hitler, and Roosevelt himself issued a vigorous statement. "The news of the past few days from Germany has deeply shocked public opinion in the United States. . . . I myself could scarcely believe that such things could occur in a twentieth century civilization."

Germany responded by recalling her ambassador, and relations thereafter remained in the hands of *chargés d'affaires*. A little later, in mid-December, Secretary Ickes of the Interior Department delivered a scorching attack upon the Nazi régime. When the German *chargé* called at the State Department to protest, he was met by Sumner Welles. Always cold and reserved, Welles is said to have been more glacially frigid than the Antarctic as he rebuked the unhappy German. His rejoinder was compressed into three icy sentences. "Protest emphatically rejected. In many decades the public opinion of the United States has not been so shocked and confounded as by recent events in Germany. Considering the language of the controlled German press towards American statesmen, this would seem to come with a singularly ill grace." That same day Senator Pittman, head of the Foreign Relations Committee, issued a public statement in which he said: "The people of the United States do not like the Government of Germany."

Meanwhile, at the eighth Pan-American Conference, held at Lima in December, 1938, the Administration was trying to build up a common front of twenty-one republics against totalitarian threats. It did not quite succeed, but it made encouraging progress towards that goal.

Secretary Hull took a carefully selected delegation to the

conference. He behaved with great tact, reasserting the pledges of non-intervention and co-operation given at previous gatherings, and insisting that he did not desire to cut the western hemisphere off from the eastern. A number of declarations were signed. They did not contain the word "democracy", for several South American Governments were not democratic; and Argentina, with her large German and Italian minorities, prevented any denunciation of totalitarianism. But the conference did adopt a declaration reaffirming the loyalty of the Americas to republicanism, and expressing their common anxiety over the new dangers to the peace of the world. They pledged themselves to consult together, if their peace, security, or territorial integrity were threatened, with a view to solidarity of action. They condemned all racial and religious persecution. Secretary Hull's favourite plan of reciprocal trade agreements was endorsed; and soon after the conference ended, the Governments of Argentina, Paraguay, Brazil, and Uruguay announced a far-reaching programme for the lowering of trade barriers.

The next European crisis was not long deferred. In March, 1939, Hitler's forces took over what remained of Czechoslovakia. In Washington the movement had been foreseen, for Minister Carr in Prague had kept Roosevelt well informed. But it filled the Administration leaders with anger. Sumner Welles is reported to have privately described it as "open thievery". Secretary Hull is said to have given free rein to his transcendent talents for picturesque profanity. Roosevelt and his Cabinet resolved to take what punitive steps they could. They hastily used some handy existing evidence of German dumping to apply countervailing duties against German goods; they instantly abrogated the trade agreement with Czechoslovakia; and they froze the Czech balances in American banks in order to reduce the German loot. Welles gave out a statement attacking the "wanton lawlessness" of Hitler's course. Declaring that the United States would not recognize the new status of Czechoslovakia, he spoke of the "temporary extinguishment of her liberties". Public approval of these acts was clearly manifested.

In April, Mussolini's invasion of Albania presented the Administration with a further challenge—and with an opportunity that Roosevelt adroitly seized. Washington feared that a general European war was about to break out. Reports came that seven German divisions had been massed on the Polish frontier. Italian military classes of 1910 and 1914 were called to the colours. Ambassador Bullitt in Paris cabled that French officials thought the chances ten to one that Hitler would begin war immediately, while the democracies were still ill-prepared. Whether a conflict was actually imminent we may not know for years to come; but Roosevelt believed that it was. He was anxious to take some step to defer it. He also perceived that he could use the situation to place the dictators clearly in the wrong; to advertise to the whole American people that they were bent upon a course of brutal aggression.

The result was that, devoting nearly a week to the task, he drafted an adroit personal appeal to Hitler and Mussolini. It was a most undiplomatic document, for it combined an indictment of Nazi and Fascist methods with a plea for peace. Roosevelt pointed out that three nations in Europe, and one in Africa, had recently lost their independence. China had been invaded and in large part occupied. He hoped it was not true that "Further acts of aggression" were, as many believed, being planned; and he reminded Hitler that he had said that the German Government had no desire for war. Speaking with the voice of America's strength, he asked Hitler and Mussolini to give him definite assurances of safety for the small nations of Europe and Asia. These he listed by name, beginning with Finland, Esthonia, Latvia, Lithuania, and ending with Palestine, Egypt, and Persia. Other powers, he declared, would gladly join Germany and Italy in guaranteeing these lands. Once peace was thus assured, conferences could be held for discussing disarmament and the promotion of international trade. On April 13 the messages were sent. To Hull, who doubted whether the hour had struck, Roosevelt is reported to have said: "We only just caught the boat before Munich. I don't want to miss it now."

It was obvious to Hitler and Mussolini that this nominal appeal was actually an indictment. The Italian dictator replied in a speech which described his love of peace, and asserted that he would pay no attention to "press campaigns, convivial vociferations, or Messiah-like messages"

Hitler called the Reichstag together, and in a long tirade ridiculed and denounced Roosevelt's message. But he made his real position plain by seizing the occasion to abrogate the non-aggression treaty with Poland, and the naval limitation agreement with Great Britain.

In these various acts Roosevelt and Hull, as the authors of *American White Paper* remark, were not actuated by a desire to enjoy the moral luxury of making faces. They had two larger objects in view. One was to convince Hitler and Mussolini, Ciano and Ribbentrop, that they might have to reckon with American hostility. We have noted that on one occasion Roosevelt used distinctly threatening language. "Words may be futile," he said in opening Congress on January 3, 1939, "but war is not the only means of commanding a decent respect for the opinions of mankind. There are many methods short of war . . . of bringing home to aggressor governments the sentiments of our people." The other object was to convince Americans that the rigid arms embargo was a mistake. Roosevelt and Hull were sadly aware that the action of Congress had deprived them of their strongest weapon in dealing with the dictators. While the arms embargo remained, if the Axis powers attacked Britain and France it would prevent American help from reaching the European democracies in their desperate need. The President might be interventionist, but Hitler knew that the law was isolationist.

From the beginning of 1939 Roosevelt therefore pressed more earnestly than ever for repeal of the Neutrality Act. "At the very least," he told Congress on January 3, "we can and should avoid any action, or any lack of action, which will encourage or assist an aggressor. We have learned that when we deliberately try to legislate neutrality, our neutrality laws may operate unevenly and unfairly—may actually give aid to the aggressor and deny it to the victim. The instinct of self-preservation should warn us that we ought not to let that happen any more."

Through the heads of the Senate and House committees on foreign affairs, strong pressure was brought to bear upon members of Congress. Early in 1939 the President talked with many Senators. War might begin soon, he warned them, and if it did it would directly affect the peace and safety of the United States. The immediate struggle would be for the domination of Europe, but if the Axis once controlled that continent, it would turn towards world domination. Yet his auditors were not sufficiently moved. They still hoped that war could be avoided, and if not, that the United States could keep out of it. Even as the Germans took Czechoslovakia and the Italians Albania, they remained suspicious of the President's wishes. Roosevelt and Hull had a bill drafted for repealing the embargo, but on July 11, the Senate committee voted 12 to 11 not to report it. They would not give the President the weapon for threatening the dictators which he hoped might help to prevent a war.

The authors of *American White Paper* have pictured the dramatic scene which took place when Roosevelt, in a final effort to sway obdurate Senate leaders, called a group of them to the White House. Hull was present. Roosevelt brought them to order with some solemnity. It might be proper to open the meeting with prayer, he said, for its decisions could well affect the entire globe. He rehearsed his familiar arguments, emphasizing the danger of war, and the fact that the arms embargo might encourage the dictators to begin it. Replying to one Senator, he said there was a strong possibility that war might begin before Congress met in regular session again in January, 1940. Secretary Hull also offered an exposition of his views, becoming more emotional than Roosevelt. But the grim old Senator from Idaho, William E. Borah, was plainly sceptical. Nobody could foretell what would happen, he remarked, but he believed that peace would continue, for Germany was not ready for war.

"I wish the Senator would come down to my office and read the cables," said Hull. "I'm sure he would come to the conclusion that there's far more danger of war than he thinks."

"So far as the reports in your department are concerned, I wouldn't be bound by them," Alsop and Kintner report Borah as saying. "I have my own sources of information, which on several occasions I have found more reliable than the State Department."

That arrogant assertion ended the matter. Vice-President Garner asked each Senator if he thought votes could be mustered for a repeal, and they all answered No. He turned to Roosevelt with a smile. "Well, Captain," he said, "you haven't got the votes."

At that time Hitler was possibly still uncertain whether to enlist Poland to help him attack Russia, or to make sure of Russia's assistance while he attacked Poland. But it is quite certain that he was resolved upon a war of conquest. Repeal or non-repeal of the American arms embargo would have made no difference to him. The prophecies of Roosevelt and Hull were tragically fulfilled when in September the European war began.

Immediately following the outbreak of hostilities, Roosevelt issued two proclamations, one defining American neutrality under the terms of international law, and the other complying with the Neutrality Act by prohibiting the exportation of "arms, ammunition, and implements of war" to the European belligerents, India, and Australasia. A few days later he extended the provisions of the law to South Africa and Canada, which had entered the war. The United States could not even sell arms to its closest and most cherished neighbour ! Then the President summoned Congress to meet in special session on September 21 ; and when it assembled, he delivered a forcible message on neutrality legislation—a message which events had made unanswerable.

Beginning in 1789, Roosevelt remarked, the United States had followed a policy with respect to belligerent nations which, with two notable exceptions, had been based on international law. One exception was provided by the Embargo and Non-Intercourse Acts under Jefferson. These acts had completely failed of their object. The other deviation from the sound principles of neutrality and peace through international law was furnished by the neutrality legislation of 1935 and 1937; legislation which, Roosevelt confessed, he regretted that he had signed. By it the United States had given up important rights, including the historic principle of the free navigation of the seas. But the neutrality legislation had done more than that. "It had the effect of putting land powers on the same footing as naval powers, so far as sea-borne commerce was concerned. A land power which threatened war could thus feel assured in advance that any prospective sea-power antagonist would be weakened through denial of its ancient right to buy anything anywhere. . . . Removal of the embargo is merely reverting to the sounder international practise, and pursuing in time of war as in time of peace our ordinary trade policies."

After some debate, Congress took the action desired by the Administration. The arms embargo was repealed; the cash-and-carry requirements were applied to all trade with belligerents; and the President was empowered to define war zones from which American ships could be debarred. Thus the executive was at last given a wide latitude in conducting the foreign affairs of the nation. Neither the President nor the State Department had ever been truly neutral in the contest which had rapidly developed in Europe between 1935 and 1939. But the transition from the thin pretence of neutrality which was at first maintained to the status of a non-belligerent alliance with the hard-beset democracies overseas was swift. It was a transition, too, which clearly had the support of majority opinion in the United States.

The lesson of these years as to the folly of the neutrality legislation was fairly clear. But a larger lesson could also be read in the events of the period. They went far towards vindicating the whole position of the internationalists—the position of the school which argued that the only true road to peace was by dynamic and unresting co-operation with all other lands. They proved that neutrality was really impossible once a great world struggle got under way. Neutrality had failed in 1812, even after the United States had embargoed all its commerce with Europe in an effort to remain at peace. It failed again in 1917, after Woodrow Wilson had made repeated efforts to negotiate between the belligerents and had struggled valiantly against a rising war sentiment in the United States. It failed in 1935–41, after the United States had gone to the point of surrendering maritime rights that it had once held indispensable. It seemed to far-sighted students of international affairs that a purely isolationist type of neutrality would always fail. The faith of those who maintained that collective security offered the only certain path to peace, that America must join other nations in stopping war at the source, and not merely try to hold aloof from wars once started—that faith was vindicated.

WORKING MEN'S COLLEGE LIBRARY

CHAPTER VII

THE WAR AND AFTER

"WE must be the great arsenal of democracy"—so President Roosevelt said in his fireside talk of December 30, 1940. "At no previous time has American security been so seriously threatened from without as it is today. . . . Our actions and our policy should be devoted primarily, almost exclusively, to meeting this foreign peril"—so he told Congress on January 6, 1941. "We do not accept, and will not permit, this Nazi shape of things to come. . . . The delivery of needed supplies to Britain is imperative. This can be done. It must be done. It will be done"—so he declared in May, 1941.

Yet American foreign policy was not transformed by the impact of the European war and Hitler's sweeping victories; it was simply broadened and given new impetus. As the nation moved forward to the defence of its own interests and of democracy throughout the globe, it expanded a pattern that had already been fixed by the Government. "We have instituted a policy of aid for the democracies," remarked Roosevelt in his speech of May, 1941. "This policy had its origin in the first month of the war, when I urged upon Congress to repeal the arms embargo." Actually, its origins might be traced much farther back. We can find a clear specification of all the main policies of the Government in his address to Congress at the beginning of 1939.

That address offered, in effect, three emphatic recommendations. After expatiating upon the rise of a group of powers bent upon wars of aggression, he made it plain that a bold course was necessary. First, the United States must look sternly to its own defences. Both the army and navy must be heavily increased. Second, it must do what it could to deter aggressors by steps to weaken and discourage them and to aid and encourage the states which they wished to make victims. For this "methods stronger and more effective than mere words" must be used. And third, the United States could in no event let "the new philosophies of force" invade the New World; it must hold them at bay in the old

VIII. CENTRES OF DIPLOMACY

1. WHITE HOUSE, WASHINGTON
(General Photographic Agency)

2. BRITISH EMBASSY, WASHINGTON
(Wide World Photos.)

3. AMERICAN EMBASSY, LONDON
(Fox Photos.)

WORKING MEN'S
COLLEGE
LIBRARY

One of these prescriptions—the urgent necessity of aug
menting America's defences—commanded general publi
support. Already sweeping plans had been made; for in th
fiscal year ending June 30, 1939, Congress had appropriate
£275,000,000 for the army, navy, and air force. In h
budget message Roosevelt now asked that appropriation
for the fiscal year ending June 30, 1940, be lifted t
£366,000,000; and this proved but a beginning. As th
shadow of the impending European storm grew blacker, h
asked for generous supplemental votes. For example, h
called for £75,000,000 to raise the Army Air Corps t
a strength of 6,000 airplanes—which, with half as man
authorized for the navy, would give the United States
total force of 9,000. Large sums were voted to the army t
complete the equipment of 400,000 National Guardsme
(the American Territorials). The two-ocean naval pro
gramme, much the largest in American history, was steadil
pushed forward.

General approval was also given to Roosevelt's plans fo
consolidating the republics of the hemisphere into a soli
phalanx for resistance to possible aggression. The Good
Neighbour policy and the Declaration of Lima offered
solid foundation for this undertaking. Moreover, some o
the twenty nations to the south were beginning to show fea
of Germany and draw closer to the United States. Early i
1939 the navy significantly held its manœuvres in the Carib
bean area, testing the Panama defences, and exploring th
best means of intercepting hostile moves across the Sout
Atlantic. Since German influence in Brazil had becom
alarming, the United States in March concluded a series o
agreements with that nation. Large loans and credits wer
granted in return for concessions to American holder
of Brazilian bonds and American traders. Later, credit
were given to Paraguay and Nicaragua for developin
their resources. The Mexican oil problem continued to b
handled with the greatest tact. In various ways Washingto
promoted the cultural influence of the United States an
combated the strident totalitarian propaganda in Lati
America.

Upon Roosevelt's policy of discouraging the aggresso
states a sharp fire was still concentrated by isolationis
elements. Nevertheless, he pressed forward with it, mor

and more distinctly throwing America on the side of the menaced democracies. In January, 1939, it was revealed that the Government was giving France official assistance in the purchase of Douglas bombing planes of the latest model, designed for army requirements. This was entirely legal. But it was done with great secrecy, and had it not been for the crash of a plane carrying a French officer, the public might not have learned about the matter. In June, King George VI and Queen Elizabeth visited the United States, made a happy impression, and were given a reception by Government officers designed to advertise the strength of Anglo-American ties. In that month also the American and British Governments signed a compact by which 600,000 bales of cotton were exchanged for 80,000 tons of rubber, both to be stored as war reserves. It was noted that during the spring Hull signed a reciprocal trade agreement—his twenty-first—with Turkey, thus strengthening a nation aligned with the anti-fascist group in Europe.

The outbreak of war abroad intensified the energy with which the Government pursued all three of its main lines of policy. Expenditures upon defence were soon trebled and quadrupled. Upon this head it is sufficient to say that the United States took steps to complete its two-ocean navy, powerful enough to deal with any enemy in the Atlantic and Pacific, by 1945; and that it set about equipping and training an air force of the first rank. Its appropriations in 1940-41 were staggering, and necessitated the raising of the debt limit from £11,250,000,000 to £16,250,000,000. Step after step was meanwhile taken to assist the democracies in Europe and Asia, and to manifest hostility towards Germany. The bonds between the United States and Latin America were drawn still closer, while Canada was made part of a virtual hemispheric union.

From the outset American opinion was overwhelmingly on the side of Britain and France. The fundamental antipathy of a democratic people for a totalitarian state had been intensified by the brutalities of the Nazi régime, its callous denial of all civil liberties, and its repeated breaches of international faith. When Roosevelt proclaimed governmental neutrality he explicitly said that he did not expect Americans to remain neutral in thought and sympathy. They did not. Yet the great majority were determined to keep out of the war if they could, and large numbers thought of the conflict as one of power politics rather than of light against darkness. Distrust of the Chamberlain and Daladier Ministries was widespread. Poland seemed far away, and American interests little involved. For a time Roosevelt himself seems to have believed that a negotiated peace might be possible. In December, 1939, he named Myron C. Taylor as his personal representative at the Vatican in order that, as he wrote the Pope, "our parallel endeavours for peace and the alleviation of suffering may be assisted". Two months later he detailed Sumner Welles to visit all the chief belligerent powers and report on "present conditions in Europe".

But the tremendous events of May and June, 1940, changed the national temper as it had changed in 1861 after Fort Sumter and in 1917 after the renewal of submarine warfare. The American people gazed in horror as Holland and Belgium were savagely overrun, France was struck down, and the Nazis left masters of the continent. They realized for the first time that the western hemisphere itself was in deadly peril from the totalitarian onslaught. The accession of Winston Churchill to power and the magnificent rally of the British people behind him stirred America profoundly. The Prime Minister's speeches—his proclamation that he had nothing to offer but blood, toil, sweat, and tears, and his declaration that Britain would wage war to the end against "a monstrous tyranny never surpassed in the dark and lamentable catalogue of human crime"—moved American feeling like a trumpet-call. Isolationist voices like Lindbergh's were still heard. But the nation pushed forward with a new unanimity to perfect its defences, to bring the whole hemisphere behind it, and to carry aid to Britain in her desperate struggle.

Under the leadership of Panama, but the obvious inspiration of the United States, the twenty-one American republics immediately after the German invasion of Holland and Belgium drew up an indictment of that act as "unjustifiable and cruel", and urged the establishment of law and justice among peoples. When Italy attacked France, Roosevelt delivered an angry speech at Charlottesville, Va.: "The hand that held the dagger has struck it into the back of its neighbour". On July 10 he asked Congress to vote £1,212,000,000 more for national defence. And in the next six months the country under his leadership took a series of steps unprecedented in history.

The President began by forming a truly national Cabinet, inviting two distinguished Republicans, Henry L. Stimson and Frank Knox, to be secretaries of war and the navy respectively. On June 19 the Government sent Germany and Italy a warning to keep hands off British, French, and Dutch possessions in the New World. In August, after Roosevelt and Prime Minister Mackenzie King had conferred, it was announced that they would at once set up a Permanent Joint Board on Defence, to "consider in a broad sense the defence of the north half of the Western Hemisphere". This practically effected a military and naval alliance of the United States and Canada—the first alliance in American history since that with France during the Revolution. That same month the President concluded an arrangement with the British Government by which fifty over-age destroyers were exchanged for 99-year leaseholds on military and naval bases in Newfoundland, Bermuda, various West Indian Islands, and British Guiana. Announced on September 3, the transaction was received with general applause. Meanwhile, Congress was considering the first peace-time conscription law in American history—the Burke–Wadsworth Selective Service Bill, which, finally signed on September 16, made about 16,500,000 men liable to enrolment for possible military training. By a system like a lottery, about 900,000 men from this group were drafted into the army for a year's service. The original act provided that this number should be trained every year for five years. In August 1941 Congress agreed to extend the period of service by eighteen months to avoid the danger of the United States being left with few trained troops under arms. Finally, the American people showed their alertness to the crisis by breaking in November, for the first time, the long tradition that no President should serve for more than two terms, and continuing Roosevelt in the White House for another four years.

The Presidential canvass had shown no real division on foreign policy. To be sure, the Republican platform had condemned Roosevelt for "explosive utterances . . . which tend to imperil the peace", and for executive acts which might lead to war without Congressional authorization.

I (N.)

But it had declared its sympathy with the struggling democracies, and called for the extension of such aid as was not in contravention of international law or inconsistent with home requirements. The Republican nominee, Wendell Willkie, endorsed all the President's measures for strengthening national defence and aiding Great Britain, criticizing him only for not going far enough. As the campaign drew to a close Roosevelt announced that American policy comprehended the defence of the hemisphere and the adjacent oceans; continued war aid to Britain on the fullest scale; insistence on the right of peaceful commerce to unrestricted use of the Atlantic and Pacific; and opposition to any peace of appeasement with the dictators. Probably four-fifths of the population endorsed every item in this programme.

The programme for bringing the American republics into a solid block met with more success than might have been expected in view of Argentine hesitations, Mexican and Chilean radicalism, and the fascist utterances of President Vargas of Brazil, a dictator of the purest water. In accordance with the Declaration of Lima, foreign ministers of all the republics assembled for consultation at Panama City soon after the war began. They adopted a statement of cooperative neutrality, defining their rights and privileges in a world at war. What was more important, they drew up the Declaration of Panama, which asserted their inherent right to keep the waters used for normal inter-American maritime communications "free from the commission of any hostile act by any non-American belligerent". For this purpose, they charted a strip extending an average distance of 300 miles from shore from the Canadian borders to the tip of Cape Horn; and they agreed to seek belligerent recognition of this zone while patrolling it to collect information on hostile craft. When the *Graf Spee* was attacked by British ships and sunk at the mouth of the River Plate, the twenty-one republics protested to Britain and Germany against fighting within the safety-zone. But the British Government replied that before consenting to the zone, it would want assurances that the area was kept neutral in fact as well as theory, and that the Pan-American proposal should not establish a precedent for far-reaching alterations in international maritime law.

As the outbreak of war brought the Panama gathering, so

the collapse of France brought a new meeting at Havana in July, 1940. Its most important work was the Act of Havana —an act which went far towards superseding the Monroe Doctrine. This was an effort to safeguard British, French, and Dutch possessions in the western hemisphere from Nazi seizure. If threatened, these possessions were to be taken over by the American republics and administered collectively until they could be organized as autonomous states, or restored to their previous status—"whichever of these alternatives shall appear the more practicable and just". An emergency committee was set up, and provision made for action by a single nation if the emergency required it. The Havana delegates also adopted a declaration that "any attempt on the part of a non-European state against the integrity or inviolability of the territory, the integrity or political independence of an American state", should be considered an act of aggression against *all* the New World republics. The Monroe Doctrine was fast becoming a multinational doctrine.

"All aid to Britain short of war"—such was the slogan of both parties during the presidential canvass. But once the election was over the qualifying phrase was dropped. Willkie on the Republican side, Roosevelt and his associates on the Democratic, were for all aid to Britain even at the risk of imminent war. To stint the aid, as they pointed out, was to run a far greater risk; for if Germany overthrew Great Britain and so gained mastery of the Atlantic, war would be certain, and a war fought against fearful odds. It was on the basis of this incontrovertible argument that Roosevelt in the first days of 1941 proposed the Lend-Lease Bill, that Congress by overwhelming majorities passed it, and that the government provided £1,750,000,000 to give it effect. The government was armed with power to manufacture or procure "any defence article" for itself or Great Britain; to sell, transfer, lease, lend, exchange, or otherwise dispose of these articles to Britain; to test, inspect, prove, repair, outfit, recondition, or otherwise place in good order any defence article—a clause under which British warships were soon being repaired in American yards; and to communicate to Britain information pertaining to any defence article—a clause under which American and British devices and ideas were soon being pooled. The terms and conditions under which this aid was extended were to be "those which the President deems satisfactory".

As aid flowed over the sea in increasing volume—"every ounce and every ton of munitions and supplies that we can possibly spare" declared Roosevelt in his fireside talk of December 30, 1940—the American and British efforts were increasingly integrated. Winston Churchill had spoken wisely when he said on August 20: "These two great organizations of the English-speaking democracies, the British Empire and the United States, will have to be somewhat mixed up together in some of their affairs for mutual and general advantage. . . . I do not view the process with misgivings. No one can stop it. Like the Mississippi, it just keeps rolling along. Let it roll. Let it roll on in full flood, inexorable, irresistible, to broader lands and better days."

The Roosevelt policy, though approved by the vast majority of the American people, was violently attacked. Some of its critics argued that the American people was being induced to waste its resources in a lost cause; the British Empire and the survival of an independent Britain were aims now impossible to attain. Others argued that peace by "mediation" was possible, that somehow, somewhere, there were possibilities of a negotiated peace. Until Russia was invaded Communists and Communist-dominated organizations denounced both parties to this "second imperialist war", an attitude that helped Germany, whatever the objective attitude of its sponsors may have been. Few Americans of any standing dared openly admit that they rejoiced in the prospect of a German victory, although the most effective leader of the isolationists, Mr. Lindbergh, had preserved none of his father's democratic biases except his dislike of intervention in European wars. But the support won by such bodies as the "America First" committee was increasingly obviously coming from German and Italian and Irish Americans, more openly based on anti-Semitism, more openly a denial of the thesis that America should be indifferent to the European issues. The noisy minority that applauded Senators Wheeler and Nye, Colonel Lindbergh and General Wood, Father Coughlin and Archbishop Beckman, was not reconciled reluctantly to a victory of the fascist powers: it welcomed the "wave of the future", the end of the liberal order, of "Jewish demoplutocracy". And the German–Russian war awoke the religious scruples of many to whom religion meant envy, malice and all uncharitableness. The American people was not slow to note that under the banner of "America First" there marched hordes of men and women, already prepared in temper to see the bright side of the triumphant denial in Europe and Asia of those principles to which the American nation was dedicated. And no nation, in a crisis, is less tolerant of divided allegiance than the American.

By the spring of 1941 the two nations were acting together for the defence of the North Atlantic. The United States had transferred more warships to Great Britain; it had set up a great patrol system on the sea-lanes leading from American ports; it had taken over the protection of Greenland. In July it was announced that the United States in agreement with Britain and the Icelandic government had occupied that great and strategically important island— hitherto thought to be decidedly in the eastern hemisphere. The Canadian–American Defence Board had held repeated meetings and drawn up numerous plans for joint action by the Dominion and the United States. American bombers were being flown in a steady and thickening stream across the sea to British air-fields, frequently making the trip in seven to nine hours. The St. Lawrence Waterways Project was being pushed forward partly as a commercial artery, partly as an item in the defence programme. British experts were poured into Washington, and American experts into London, to co-ordinate the work of Britain, Canada, and America in a dozen diverse fields.

In the Caribbean and Latin America the same unity obtained. The bases handed over by Britain in Jamaica, the Bahamas, St. Lucia, Antigua, Trinidad, and British Guiana made a chain that was invaluable for the protection of the Panama Canal and the northern flank of South America. Great Britain had approved the Act of Havana. America was policing the waters of Martinique and Guadeloupe to keep an eye on naval vessels and gold still controlled by Vichy France. Both Washington and London felt distinct uneasiness over the economic position of South America. The British blockade of Europe had cost many of the republics their best customers. More than half the food exported from Latin America in 1938 had gone to Europe, and some nations had sent seventy to ninety per cent of their produce. Antagonism to the blockade was natural, and under other circumstances Germany might have exploited it. But the United States was taking action to buy up part of the unused surpluses, and to quiet discontent in other ways.

Still more marked was the parallelism between British and American policy in the Far East. Roosevelt in his speeches repeatedly emphasized the determination of the United States to assist China to maintain her independence. In July, 1940, Washington took fresh steps to impede Japan in her aggressions. It prohibited the export of petroleum and its products and of scrap metal without specific licence; and it completely banned the export of aviation gasolene to countries outside the Western Hemisphere. Against this ban Japan immediately protested. It was no mere coincidence that a similar ban was laid on the export of scrap iron on October 15, almost the same day that Britain reopened the Burma Road. Nor was it a mere coincidence that after the United States on November 30 loaned China £25,000,000, the British Government on December 11 gave her credits of £10,000,000. While Britain was feverishly reinforcing Singapore, the American Congress was voting large sums to strengthen Manila and Hawaii, and to fortify Guam and Samoa. It was clear by the spring of 1941 that the British and American naval commands in the Pacific had more than a general understanding as to possible co-operation in joint action.

A great Anglo-American union for the winning of the war between the totalitarian states and the democracies had, in short, taken shape. It was a completely informal union, and not an alliance. It was in the main simply an out-growth of that American principle which we have mentioned as of cardinal importance at all times in the conduct of foreign affairs: the principle of supporting democracy throughout the globe. But it was a union that would not easily be dissolved. Even if the two nations did not wish to do so, they could not avoid a partnership in making the peace, and in seeing it preserved afterward. President Roosevelt on March 16, 1941, had given a significant pledge: "Our country must continue to play its great part in the period of world reconstruction for the good of

IX. THE ATLANTIC MEETING

1. MR. CHURCHILL AND MR. ROOSEVELT ON H.M.S. "PRINCE OF WALES"
2. BRITISH AND AMERICAN SAILORS ON THE "PRINCE OF WALES"

(Crown Copyright Reserved)

WORKING MEN'S
COLLEGE
LIBRARY

humanity." The announcement made on August 14 that
the President of the United States and the Prime Minister
of Great Britain had met in the Atlantic stirred popular
imagination on both sides of the ocean. But although the
immediate problems of policy which were discussed could
only be guessed at, certain of the decisions taken underlined
the determination of the President to throw America's
weight effectually against the Axis. The offer of war material to Russia was one proof of this determination. But it
was not only war that was discussed. By a joint declaration the two statesmen not only set up a standard to which
men of good will in all countries could rally, they made it
plain that they, at least, would not commit the mistake of
1919–1920. There would be no falling back into the comfortable and slothful and deadly illusion that "victory would
keep". There was on the part of Mr. Roosevelt and Mr.
Churchill a proclamation of the truth that only by brave
and continued effort, lasting long after the formal ending of
the war, only by a resumption of the neglected task of world
organization, could "life, liberty and the pursuit of happi-
ness" be made possible for the victims of Hitlerite aggression
—and for the German people themselves. Close cooperation in war and peace was being forced on the two great
English-speaking nations by the crude revelation of the
Nazi designs to organize the world on a basis of tyranny and
plunder. On the basis of the solid understanding of all the
English-speaking peoples, men could indeed look forward
to broader lands and better days.

WORKING MEN'S COLLEGE
LIBRARY

TEXT OF THE JOINT DECLARATION

The President of the United States and the Prime Minister, Mr. Churchill, representing his Majesty's Government in the United Kingdom, being met together, deem it right to make known certain common principles in the national policies of their respective countries on which they base their hopes for a better future for the world.

FIRST, their countries seek no aggrandisement, territorial or other.

SECOND, they desire to see no territorial changes that do not accord with the freely expressed wishes of the peoples concerned.

THIRD, they respect the right of all peoples to choose the form of Government under which they will live ; and they wish to see sovereign rights and self-government restored to those who have been forcibly deprived of them.

FOURTH, they will endeavour, with due respect for their existing obligations, to further enjoyment by all States, great or small, victor or vanquished, of access, on equal terms, to the trade and to the raw materials of the world which are needed for their economic prosperity.

FIFTH, they desire to bring about the fullest collaboration between all nations in the economic field, with the object of securing for all, improved labour standards, economic advancement, and social security.

SIXTH, after the final destruction of Nazi tyranny, they hope to see established a peace which will afford to all nations the means of dwelling in safety within their own boundaries, and which will afford assurance that all the men in all the lands may live out their lives in freedom from fear and want.

SEVENTH, such a peace should enable all men to traverse the high seas and oceans without hindrance.

EIGHTH, they believe all of the nations of the world, for realistic as well as spiritual reasons, must come to the abandonment of the use of force. Since no future peace can be maintained if land, sea, or air armaments continue to be employed by nations which threaten, or may threaten, aggression outside of their frontiers, they believe, pending the establishment of a wider and permanent system of general security, that the disarmament of such nations is essential. They will likewise aid and encourage all other practicable measures which will lighten for peace-loving peoples the crushing burden of armaments.

INDEX

PRINTED IN GREAT BRITAIN BY RICHARD CLAY AND COMPANY, LTD.,
BUNGAY, SUFFOLK.

WORKING MEN'S
COLLEGE
LIBRARY

WORKING MEN'S COLLEGE
CROWNDALE ROAD, N.W.

19 MAY 1953

24 OCT 1958

WORKING MEN'S COLLEGE,
CROWNDALE ROAD, N.W.

THIS BOOK TO BE RETURNED BY:

WORKING MEN'S COLLEGE,
CROWNDALE ROAD, N.W.